The Bauxite
Strike
and the
Old Politics

for Sister Karen
with love & Respect
Eusi Kwayana
October 8, 2012

By Eusi Kwayana

With a new introduction by
Matthew Quest

The Bauxite Strike and the Old Politics

Copyright © 2012 by Eusi Kwayana

This edition is published by
On Our Own Authority! Publishing,
Atlanta, Georgia

OooA! online:
www.oooabooks.org

Email us:
contact@oooaboooks.org

Cover design for this edition by:
Allison Specketer
www.allisonspecketer.viewbook.com

Originally Printed in 1972 by
Bovell's Printery, Georgetown, Guyana
with cover design volunteered by
Ms. Megan Anderson.

ISBN-13: 978-0-9858909-0-2
ISBN-10: 0-985-89090-8

Contents

Praise for Eusi Kwayana's
The Bauxite Strike and the Old Politics

"Eusi Kwayana's, *The Bauxite Strike and the Old Politics* is a classic document of the Caribbean New Left and of the region's still unborn post-colonial political imagination. This re-issuing will therefore be of great interest to scholars of the Caribbean New Left Movements…and other movements of worker liberation and empowerment. Very nicely re-introduced by Matthew Quest, the work makes clear the strong claims these movements made regarding the self-organizing capabilities of workers. Further, it sheds great light on the roots of the post-colonial crisis of governance in the region, which has only gotten worse since the time during which Kwayana wrote this penetrating text. A must read for all who are thinking about the rebuilding of a global Left movement."

— Paget Henry, Sociology and Africana Studies, Brown University, Author of *Caliban's Reason: Introducing Afro-Caribbean Philosophy*

"The republication of Eusi Kwayana's *Bauxite Strike and the Old Politics*…could not be more welcome forty years after its first introduction and impact. In a state of affairs in Guyana today where the 'old politics' is very much alive, Kwayana's [work]…is as relevant as ever."

— Nigel Westmaas, Africana Studies Department, Hamilton College, USA.

"The new edition of Eusi Kwayana's *The Bauxite Strike and the Old Politics*…is a well-written account of struggles against injustice, oppression and corruption in Guyana's post-independence era. Undoubtedly, *The Bauxite Strike and the Old Politics* will serve to enlighten this generation of forgotten snippets of Caribbean history…"

— Jerome Teelucksingh, History Department, University of the West Indies, Trinidad and Tobago.

From Party Politics to Popular Committees of Labor and the Landless in Guyana

An Introduction by Matthew Quest

Eusi Kwayana's *The Bauxite Strike and the Old Politics* chronicles events more than forty years old. Far more than has been realized, this book speaks to the world in which we now live. A classic of Caribbean political thought, it speaks to dilemmas of American and global civilization. A product of Guyana, a land distinguished by heroic moments of multiracial politics as well as racial insecurity, and the only Anglophone speaking nation in South America, it mirrors a turning point in Black and Pan-African History on a world scale.

A story of labor revolt, it is an occasion for reconsidering how we understand anti-racist and post-colonial politics. During the events of the bauxite strike, popular councils and committees began to emerge, representing the potential of workers self-management at the expense of state power. Through the text we witness a movement toward the rejection of electoral party politics and their inherent suppression of labor's potential to achieve self-emancipation and new forms of freedom.

This is also a story of how Black Power activists began to come to terms with the centrality of the self-emancipation of Black labor as the basis for Black autonomy, which stands in distinct contrast to elite party politics and a Black led state power. Since the early 1970s, aspiring liberation movements and opponents of white supremacy have never quite recovered from the incapacity to comprehend the eventual reconversion of state power, in imperial and formerly colonized nations, toward an ethnic pluralism, which increasingly repudiated historical abuses, but led to the strengthening of the empire of capital, and the disorientation of anti-racist struggles.

In this historical moment, those acting in solidarity with the self-organization of Black labor posed a necessary break with the claims to legitimacy of Black progressive ruling elites. More broadly, these events serve to inspire a rethinking of the limits of representative government.

Just as it was necessary to ask which social class led the national liberation struggle, it also became indispensable to inquire under what terms a government should be constituted that could ensure an ethical independence and self-reliance. Black middle class elements in Guyana—credibly on one level—denounced racism, poverty, inequality, and empire, as they aspired to seize power, enter the rules of hierarchy, and establish themselves as a "progressive" ruling elite. In years prior, nearly all Black Power activist voices seemed to have paved the way for the ascendancy of this class. In the face of this history, it took tremendous acts of courage to rethink how vistas of Black autonomy had historically contributed to the surfacing of these (as termed by the famous Guyanese poet, Martin Carter) "shining governments of the damned." Eusi Kwayana is distinguished by that type of audacity but also a humble self-criticism.

Notes on the Life of Eusi Kwayana

As an activist and school teacher, Kwayana promoted a popular understanding of Guyana's history, with a particular emphasis on the Berbice Rebellion of 1763 and the Free Village Movement of 1831-1852, which, to Kwayana, reveal an often unacknowledged truth—that wisdom is plentiful among ordinary people in their capacity for self-emancipation.

A Pan-African and independent socialist, a dynamic innovator as a cultural nationalist, and facilitator of class struggle, Kwayana has been perceived as a protean and mystical figure at home and abroad. This is partially a result of his shifting allegiances in Guyana's politics, his criticism of vanity and vanguard leadership personalities, and the matter that his vast archive of writings have never been widely distributed in metropolitan centers and research libraries. Even among Black Power and Pan-African activists, who traveled in his circles of influence, there was an underdeveloped engagement with the textual record of his ideas. Nevertheless, he has been central to almost every major democratic and anti-colonial movement in Guyana in the second half of the twentieth century, and has been a teacher of popular national history. For those not familiar with Eusi Kwayana, his life has been inextricably linked to the triumvirate of personalities that have come to define modern politics in Guyana: Cheddi Jagan, Forbes Burnham, and Walter Rodney.

In 1947-1953, Eusi Kwayana (as Sydney King) was part of the movement for colonial independence, and was later a minister of state in Guyana's first transitional government, led by the Marxist People's Progressive Party (PPP) of Cheddi Jagan and Forbes Burnham. The British later toppled that regime, and Kwayana became a political prisoner in 1953. When, subsequently, Forbes Burnham split with Cheddi Jagan to form the overwhelmingly Afro-Guyanese People's National Congress (PNC), Kwayana remained with Jagan until 1957. His split with Jagan took place over the issue that Jagan appeared, to Kwayana, as not desiring to challenge his overwhelming Indo-Guyanese base to adopt a more multiracial organizational practice. Kwayana also took issue with Jagan's rejection of Guyana joining the movement for Caribbean Federation. In his pamphlet *Next Witness* (1962),[1] Kwayana argued the Indo-Guyanese politician Cheddi Jagan, (who nationally and internationally held prestige as a socialist politician affiliated with Moscow) passively accepted racial chauvinism toward Afro-Guyanese among ordinary Indo-Guyanese in ethnically separate neighborhoods. This insight was crucial in explaining past

---

1   Sydney King. (Eusi Kwayana) *Next Witness: An Appeal to World Opinion.* Georgetown, Guyana: Labour Weekly, 1962.

conservative cracks and future radical ruptures in this national liberation movement.

Kwayana was a central figure in the racial conflicts of 1961-1964 which fractured the relationship between Afro-Guyanese and Indo-Guyanese. Based on his analysis in *Next Witness*, and in the face of ugly, divisive, and increasingly frequent race riots of 1963 and 1964, Kwayana promoted the need for joint premiership and power sharing, with racial partition of the country considered as a last resort. Kwayana argued that Guyana should be partitioned—not so much along racial lines, but along the two major parties' ethnic spheres of influence. Critics of this plan would always minimize that part of this vision of partition would also be to create a multiracial sector where those who wished to live in harmony could do so freely.

ASCRIA and the PNC

In 1964, Kwayana cofounded ASCRIA (The African Society for Cultural Relations with Independent Africa), which, like its predecessor ASRE (The African Society for Racial Equality), was dedicated to the promotion, among Afro-Guyanese, of prideful identification with African culture and colonial independence on the African continent. It was during his time serving as Coordinating Elder, or chief spokesperson, of ASCRIA that he converted his identity from Sydney King to Eusi Kwayana, which in Kiswahili translates to "Black Man of Guyana." As coordinating elder of ASCRIA, he was an originator of the direct democratic current of the Caribbean New Left from 1970-1974.

During the 1964 elections, ASCRIA gave full support to the PNC, playing a central role in mobilizing election support within Guyana. They promoted to Afro-Guyanese that the Burnham government would address the masses' needs by crafting a cooperative republic, and these would be satisfied with minimal corruption. Later, ASCRIA promoted to Africans abroad that a Burnham led Guyana was a refuge to the oppressed where institutions were being created to satisfy people's economic stresses. But by 1973, ASCRIA announced a definitive break with the PNC, viewing its leaders as exploiters of the workers and farmers, and plunderers of public resources, almost without exception. The perspective was that as the PNC leaders gained more power, they became more arrogant, corrupt, and callous as they formed links with American imperialism and the Bookers Sugar Corporation.

ASCRIA began as the facilitators of a cultural front for Burnham's PNC. Following the example of CLR James' *Party Politics in the West Indies,* they desired to promote a type of "cultural revolution." Through fastening a cultural front to the PNC led state, ASCRIA taught the progressive masses loyal to the PNC about liberation politics and the goals of a social and economic revolution.

ASCRIA preached collectivism and socialism, or what in Tanzania was termed "ujamaa." Those within the PNC fold who did not learn aspects of revolutionary politics from ASCRIA were learning the terms of patronage and leaders' power from the Burnham hierarchy.

ASCRIA promoted aspects of direct democracy and advised toilers about the power of their self-organization in their workplaces, while at the same time strove to advise the Burnham government about the potential of the self-mobilized people for progressive policy initiatives above society. Beginning by promoting dynamic aspects of national culture for self-reliance, ASCRIA increasingly took the side of self-managing workers in their rebellion against the state, which seemed the logical culmination of a national liberation struggle wherein the Guyana government had nationalized property.

Later, Kwayana split with Burnham while still maintaining critical support for his PNC, and recommending a multi-racial solution to the problems of Guyana. *The Bauxite Strike* is a record of Kwayana's activism, on the heels of the gravest era of racial insecurity in Guyana, where he began to foment class struggle against Forbes Burnham's regime which came to power in 1966. Remarkable in ASCRIA's evolution was not merely their criticism of the Burnham government, but their public self-criticism which framed their evolving positions as mirroring the growing consciousness of the Guyanese working people.

What are "the Old Politics?"

Before discussing the details of the labor actions which inform Eusi Kwayana's *The Bauxite Strike and the Old Politics*, let us identify and examine the fossilized politics of which the author wishes to dispose. On the frontispiece of this volume are three quotes. Lenin's "every cook must learn to govern" shows the influence of CLR James' thoughts on both Lenin and the Ancient Athenian direct democracy, which he lectured about to a mass audience in Guyana in 1966. An Akan proverb from Ghana is offered: "The sayings of the poor are not quoted." Finally, a Guyanese proverb: " 'Tone deh a bottam ribba e na know ow sun 'at." Thus, ruling elites do not know or can not see the potential at the bottom of society's metaphorical "river." The common people's source of light or wisdom is known to be plentiful at the bottom, for those that possess the proper way of seeing. It is with this wisdom that ordinary people can govern society. Another interpretation could assert that the ruling elite, who live a leisurely life soothed by cool waters of the river, know not the sweat and toil under the hot sun of the ordinary laborer.

Similar to James' *Party Politics in the West Indies*[2], which chides Trinidad's Eric Williams for his inability or lack of desire to cultivate the Caribbean popular will properly toward a more full national

---

2   CLR James. *Party Politics in the West Indies.* San Juan, Trinidad: Vedic, 1962.

liberation where "politics is an activity" enhancing what the state can do, Kwayana's *The Bauxite Strike* clarifies the origins of corruption. The "old politics" is the neglect of a national liberation parties' responsibility to be agents of mass mobilization, offering education for social reconstruction and functioning as a new public morality. Instead, these post-colonial rulers concerned themselves only with mobilization for electoral victory and maintaining their own authority. This proves shaky ground for aspiring rulers whom, under the pressures of the self-mobilization of ordinary people, underestimate or ignore their efforts.

Thus Kwayana, disinterested in any aspiration of personal power, presents *The Bauxite Strike and the Old Politics*, partially as an offering to aid Forbes Burnham as a "supporter" of his nationalization of Guyana's key economic centers, by advising Burnham that his approach to party politics must be reformed. Just as CLR James advised Eric Williams in Trinidad, if Burnham chooses not to act as a facilitator and patron for workers that take industrial action, he has no choice but to ultimately outlaw their activities and subsequently use state power to crush their efforts at self-mobilization. Kwayana advises Burnham that would be both barbaric and against the nation's interests.

Yet, on the lower frequencies, Eusi Kwayana's *The Bauxite Strike* raises a new kind of politics for Guyana. Under the premise of asking Burnham's PNC to share self-criticism of his rule with rebellious bauxite workers, Kwayana raises the banner of an alternative vision toward implementation of nationalization of industry—direct democracy and workers self-management as the embodiment of national purpose.

The Bauxite Strike and the Old Politics abounds with original insights by Kwayana, and the bauxite mine workers themselves, on the validity of direct democratic processes. But it is also most remarkable for two critical claims that CLR James himself would rarely suggest, at least about Caribbean politics. During the events of the bauxite labor actions we will shortly discuss, Kwayana is self-critical that he was insufficiently confident in the workers' self-governing capacities, and at times they were themselves. Further, he asserts that there are limitations to how far a direct democracy may be facilitated through popular assemblies. We will sum up these insights and limitations to popular self-management after a brief review of the labor actions surrounding the bauxite strike in Guyana.

Strikes in the Bauxite Industry

Bauxite, a mineral used in the production of aluminum, is vital to the aerospace, automobile, and electronics industries. Bauxite mining itself involves a series of dredges, drag lines, and heavy duty machinery in the removal of "overburden," or topsoil composed of sand and silt, facilitating retrieval of the bauxite. The bauxite, after being transported to the factory via railroad car, would then be processed. This involves washing the ore in boiling sulfuric acid (at temperatures reaching over 300 degrees), which strips the bauxite of its iron residue before it is dried in a kiln (heated to over 2000 degrees), thus creating a grey white powder, known as alumina. In this form, it is sent abroad to be converted into various metallic products. This was a dangerous labor process where workers in the factory, particularly the filtration operators, used protective goggles, long boots, gloves and other gear. Occasionally there were grave accidents on the job where coworkers were permanently burned and scarred. [3]

The bauxite workers struggled in the company town of Wismar-MacKenzie (Linden). During colonial times, one needed a pass to cross the Demerara River, which divided these twin cities. Even after independence, the colonial mentality remained in the expatriate managerial class. Overwhelmingly white, they lived

---

3   Frank Richmond, interviewed by author: Spring, 2012

racially segregated in Richmond Hills and Watooka (East bank of MacKenzie). Early struggles of the bauxite workers against racism and sexism took place among workshops where tools and die makers were stored, and within the private hospital and segregated cinema of the company town.[4]

In early, post-colonial, Guyana, bauxite mining was a major industry which was transitioning from ownership by multinational corporations to the status of nationalized, "public" property. Black workers who previously led strikes against racism, sexism, and disputes with white managers around benefits packages, began to face the ultimate confrontation of striking against their own, elected, post-colonial government. Forbes Burnham's People's National Congress believed once the Guyana government, with its Pan African trappings, owned the bauxite industry, the Black workers would accept his mediation as acting in their best interests.

Throughout the 1960s, wildcat strikes were pervasive in confronting the abuses of ALCAN, a Canadian firm that owned the Demerara Bauxite Company (DEMBA) and was known for discrimination against Black workers. In 1970, popular uprisings began in the bauxite mines of Linden (Wismar-MacKenzie), and it was largely perceived that the Guyana Mine Workers Union (GMWU) had failed to adequately represent the toilers, and was a union loyal to the corporation. Later, after nationalization, the GMWU showed loyalty to the new management, Burnham's government.

Direct action against DEMBA was not centrally directed by ASCRIA, but rather by a local affiliate. The local ASCRIA chapter was involved in four labor actions in the years 1966 to 1971 involving issues of racism towards black workers and professionals employed by DEMBA, and in the face of GMWU paralysis.

---

4   Ibid.

These initial rebellions, coordinated by ASCRIA and aimed at ALCAN, received little response from the PNC-led regime. Yet, with the nationalization of industry in 1971, there were sweeping adjustments of the state's disposition to such matters. DEMBA, owned by ALCAN and operating out of Linden, was the first to be purchased and "owned by the public." Burhham's state, upon seizing control of the company, now had to negotiate with ASCRIA, an ally who previously offered critical support. The GMWU, whose leadership transparently collaborated with ALCAN, now shifted toward a loyal opposition to the government. Burnham's regime now had to deal directly with the complaints of workers who previously were perceived as faithful devotees of the PNC.

Frank Richmond, known as "Frank Abel," was an original member of "The Committee of Ten," which he defined as a "leaderless group," and which was the forerunner of the Organization of Working People, based in Linden. It was his circle which published *Voice of the Workers*. Part of the RILA dispute, Richmond observed that the PNC government seized ALCAN's matched contributions to workers' retirement funds, and only offered to pay interest on these savings, which had been placed aside by the workers themselves. The matched funds, originally contributed by ALCAN, seemed to have been stolen after nationalization.[5]

In April 1971, the RILA strike was an epic showdown between bauxite miners and their employer, which was now the Guyanese government. Animated by concerns for wage increases and desire for a renewal of the "retirement income life assurance" plan, previously maintained by DEMBA, miners desired that

---

5   Frank Richmond, interviewed by author: Spring, 2012. As a result of his activism, which challenged the authority of the government, who now owned this nationalized industry, Richmond was finally handed his letter of termination by the superintendent of the aluminum plant in 1978

their new employer, the Guyanese state under the leadership of Burham's PNC, must continue supporting this initiative on which the workers were economically dependent. After more than a year of negotiations, with no indication that a resolution was forthcoming, the labor action commenced.

Jailed and beaten by the army, strikers were subjected to tear gas in their cells by the police. In the course of the strike, 27 workers were subject to multiple charges including unlawful assembly and disorderly conduct. While regime spokespeople insisted the miners were responsible for their own rough treatment, Eusi Kwayana contested that the strikers were not opposed to the government, but were merely standing up for themselves in their workplace. The union bureaucracy, having not sanctioned the strike, suspended 20 members who they contended were the leaders of this labor action. Subsequently there was a series of legal battles over four years by "The Committee of Ten," made up of some of these punished miners to expose the unilateral and invalid extended terms of office of the leaders of the union hierarchy. The courts ultimately agreed with the blacklisted workers and repaired them to their former job status with union membership.

The government wished to divide the workers eligible for RILA pension money by refunding their investment, without contributing to it, if they had been on the job for less than twelve years. The Committee of Ten responded with a one day strike on November 7, 1971 but this action proved less powerful than the previous action in April. This was partially as a result of government threats, but also due to the fact that most of those who received the refund did not revolt. However, the state did eventually offer those miners with more than twelve years on the job the opportunity to transfer their investment into a new pension fund.

Direct Democracy and Black Power

Eusi Kwayana's *The Bauxite Strike and the Old Politics* is a kindred work, but also an extension of CLR James' arguments in *Party Politics in the West Indies*. It anticipates and elaborates vistas for Guyana that are similar to those found in another neglected text. CLR James' *The Invading Socialist Society* argues for the firm "proletarianization" of nationalized property through direct democracy by revolutionists in nations where state power has undertaken such industrial planning. This was not a stance appropriate only for modern industrial nations, but wherever peripheral nations' political economy posed the same modes of production. James asserts that at moment where a government takes up state capitalist planning as pretense toward progress, there is no crisis of revolutionary leadership, but rather of working people's own self-mobilization where they must overcome obstacles regimes put in their place, but also of their own making.[6]

The Bauxite Strike and the Old Politics, like CLR James' *Party Politics in the West Indies*, is a critique by an "insider" within party politics suggesting a breaking away from such premises. However, also similar to James' *Party Politics*, Kwayana exhibits another discourse, "politics as an activity," distinct from parliamentary and trade union bureaucratic forms.

To Kwayana, nationalization of industry was not "too revolutionary" a step. He asserts that the bauxite workers embraced nationalization in ideal "political" terms, but not "industrially." For the Black workers of Guyana were not "helped"

---

6 CLR James. (1947) With Raya Dunayevskaya and Grace Lee. *The Invading Socialist Society.* Detroit: Bewick, 1972. 53-55. It is notable that James in his preface of 1972 to this small book, at the height of the struggle in Guyana under discussion, re-emphasizes a movement for direct workers control of production through popular committees can be the only response to a state which claims to plan the economy in the name of the people.

by the PNC to see how they "fit into the new arrangements."[7]—because from the point of view of the state, they did not. At Linden, the PNC (and PPP) was "outpaced by the spontaneous organization of the people themselves." Kwayana, emphasizes firmly that the PNC had the "political loyalty" of the overwhelming majority of the workers, especially before the smashing of their strike, but not their "operational loyalty."

Eusi Kwayana gives reasons why he was not at first an enthusiastic supporter of the strike, though an ASCRIA local chapter was crucial to helping to organize it.

> The view of the April revolt taken by members of
> ASCRIA was that the strike was a mistake in view
> of the fact that the Nationalization Act had been
> passed by Parliament. It did not share the profound
> loss of confidence in the Government expressed by
> the workers on strike. As black revolutionaries, the
> members have been trained to have confidence in
> black leaders thus overcoming generations of lack
> of faith which had bedeviled our communities for
> centuries...[8]

Kwayana is, at this point, still in the process of working out an insurgent post-colonial politics where support for Black labor from below would be in conflict with Black rulers on high, deemed progressive by most. The reservations, both of ASCRIA and Kwayana (one should not always assume internal unity within ASCRIA) are reflected in the leaflets of 1970 and 1971, found in *The Bauxite Strike's* seventh chapter. Nevertheless, he argues, despite his reservations, "the members of the leadership of the revolt

---

7   Eusi Kwayana, *The Bauxite Strike and the Old Politics* (Atlanta: On Our Own Authority!, 2012), 82.

8   *The Bauxite Strike*, 88.

were serious thinkers…they tried out new forms of organization."

But Kwayana asserts, "the fact that the workers' committee filled a gap in the process of life does not say that it was the form that will best serve the new situation." Rather, he argues that the crucial importance of the bauxite strike is its exhibition of the potential of "alienated" toilers to rise against crises with "self-assertion," and the potential "for creative development of workers' government." As Kwayana observes, "Such workers are in quality ready for socialism and ready to defend it."[9]

Eusi Kwayana, alluding to CLR James' political thought, speaks of the decline of mass meetings in the imperial nations and their omnipresent nature in the Caribbean. Through public education, ordinary people learn the character of the "enemy" and the obstacles to change. In these spaces, they begin to reach agreement on how to attack and solve problems. But Kwayana recognized that these mass meetings, which could be imagined as a form of direct democracy, were called, only to be ceased at the time of elections.

In many ways, national liberation parties in Guyana were really electoral parties. The perception that ordinary people were "learning to govern" at these meetings was obscured by the fact that they were often undermined by the very party whose vision they endorsed. Once in state power, these parties have replaced mass meetings with press releases and media appearances. That is, of course, unless they are in the parliamentary opposition. While press releases may be more efficient, in certain respects, than public mass meetings which hold a finite audience, the resulting outcome is still a decline in the relationship between the political philosopher and crowd, and a degenerated conception of citizenship.

Kwayana sees the value of these meetings through the eyes

---

9   *The Bauxite Strike*, 89.

of the agitator or propagandist, who not only makes speeches but can "sense" the crowd's "questions, doubts, [and] fears" and can "learn from them," even when participants express themselves by means of heckling. Kwayana notes: "No one can talk back to a newspaper or radio broadcast." Interestingly, he also sees the public meeting that anticipates forms of popular assembly or direct democracy as having "severe limitations." "But it is unequaled as a direction giver, as a mood tester, as a solidarity builder, as a means of communication between so-called leaders and followers or supporters." However, in Kwayana's view such meetings can not replace either the "party cell or the classroom."[10]

Kwayana speaks of the bauxite strike as a historical process where perspectives actually developed over time and where "we all" learned to govern. He offers an insight CLR James would not make. For James often imagined popular committees and assemblies, as the forms of freedom for self-emancipation, as a beautiful totality. Kwayana offers an important proposition to consider. The bauxite workers at times had "extremely narrow views." There is no evidence that they rejected "the lifestyle lived by elite[s]." For Eusi Kwayana, the experience of the bauxite strike and direct democracy could not be overwhelmingly enchanted if political lessons were to be learned. However, one year later he would facilitate a rebellion of landless sugar workers which was marked not just by an instinct toward direct democracy, but also a program for popular self-management.

Landless Sugar Workers' Rebellion

The first joint popular protest that brought Afro-Guyanese and Indo-Guyanese together in mass mobilization since the struggle for independence, was the 1973 "land rebellion" led by ASCRIA. ASCRIA called for the British sugar company, Bookers, to

---

10   *The Bauxite Strike*, 95-96.

hand over unused lands to the African and Indian sugar workers. Towards this end, ASCRIA called on the people to seize the land through direct democratic means. The response to this call was profound, as Indians and Africans in communities on the East Coast of Demerara adjoining the sugar estates occupied the lands and began to implement economic plans, and judicial affairs. Popular committees were formed in each village to coordinate the campaign. Kwayana recalled: "There were four Indian bases and three African." Racial division had been an obstacle to joint action, but when the farmers heard of the "representative formula" all tensions ceased.[11] It is estimated that about 245 acres of land were occupied and approximately two thousand people participated in the campaign.

The campaign was not aimed directly at the government. Nevertheless, the PNC reacted harshly. After the first week of squatting, the government gave the squatters a 48 hour ultimatum to cease their action. When they did not comply, the police forcibly removed the squatters from the lands they occupied. Homes, in the process of being erected by the squatters, were burned by the police, and the army was alerted in the event of the need of more force. Eventually, three persons were charged with trespassing, but these charges were subsequently dismissed by the courts.

Having yet again exposed the superficial shell of nationalized property in Guyana, ASCRIA decided to call off the protest. The last day of the campaign, February 17, 1974 was designated "Day of Redemption of Sugar Lands." A group of 25 protesters fasted for 12 hours, and a community meeting attended by 600 people was held at Paradise, a village on the East Coast. There was also an all night vigil by ASCRIA members at the group's headquarters in Georgetown on the night of February 17. So effective was the campaign, that on February 23, the Prime

---

11   Eusi Kwayana. Correspondence with Author. Winter 2006.

Minister announced that the Sugar Production Association (SPA), the group that represented the sugar companies, had agreed to turn over to the government most of the unused lands.

Discovering and Seizing Sugar Lands:
ASCRIA's Direct Democratic Guidelines

The ASCRIA "Guidelines" for "discovering or seizing" sugar lands is a remarkable political document. Not a commentary on the behavior of aspiring progressive rulers, but rather a step by step guide for implementing direct democracy and popular self-management of the sugar lands through popular committees. The text (included in the appendix of this volume) is distinguished by the following qualities.

The landless are implored not to seize private property of members of the same or different ethnic group, but only historical sugar company land. Bookers had placed some land aside, in the state's hands, for the sugar workers, but never transferred these lands to the working people. ASCRIA thus advised the landless sugar workers to squat this land and negotiate for the deed on the basis that the population understood it to be the property of the nation, of which they were the popular democratic embodiment. The landless were implored to not offer even the smallest payment to authorities, and to watch the official government gazette to make sure the titles to the land were not being passed over their heads. Government ministers were attempting to offer "progressive" policies and "easy credit" so the land could be purchased by farmers, but also the state wanted to tax the land and charge for water. ASCRIA condemned these policies.

A culture of direct democracy for the popular committees was suggested. Nobody was to be left off an area committee for their party membership but anybody who attempted to impose their old party politics was to be excluded. It was imperative that these committees be allowed to discuss among themselves, with no state intervention. They were to report "fully to all the people," chronicling achievements and, just as importantly, mistakes and obstacles to self-reliance.

It was this successful multiracial rebellion of toilers which anticipated a new wave of labor action among the bauxite workers and the surfacing of the politics of Walter Rodney's Working People's Alliance.

Later: Walter Rodney, the WPA, and the OWP

Walter Rodney's[12] return to Guyana in 1974-1975 was a catalyst for solidifying what became the Working People's Alliance (originally not a political party but a network of four groups). Besides ASCRIA there were the Ratoon group, the Indian Political Revolutionary Associates, and the Working People's Vanguard Party. The WPA informally worked among the OWP bauxite workers conducting "the Bottom House University" in Wismar in 1975-1976. Walter Rodney taught economic history, emphasizing evolving modes of production from bartering to the extraction of surplus value. He surveyed economic developments in Africa, the Caribbean, the United States and Europe. Rupert Roopnarine taught about some of the social implications of English literature. Eusi Kwayana taught about the situation in the country for what it was—highlighting political and racial divisions. Responding to the PNC's racial appeals to the Black majority, Kwayana criticized Burnham for implying to Black audiences that, if he did not rule, there would be Indian supremacy. Further, if you were Black and raised a finger in protest against Burnham one would be in trouble. A multi-racial direct democratic breakthrough was required.

It is important to recognize that the bauxite workers' self-

12   Walter Rodney (1942-1980), author of *How Europe Underdeveloped Africa* (1972), assassinated by Burnham's regime in the rebellion of 1979-1980.

organization for emancipation, from the Committee of Ten to the OWP, was never a front for ASCRIA or the WPA. Bauxite workers like Frank Richmond learned much from the fellowship they received from their radical activist peers. During the height of events they did not wish to be publicly linked, as they lived a semi-underground political existence, and did not wish to be victimized by the PNC regime and lose their jobs. Comrades in strike activity would often, seeing each other at a distance, turn down another street, so as not to be even seen greeting each other in public. Yet the bauxite workers, ASCRIA, and WPA activists were tremendous assets to each other.

Frank Richmond recalls that, during these years of struggle, he initially saw Pan African ideas and class struggle as related visions, but he had accepted that post-colonial leaders spoke on behalf of the working class. Through a process of critical reflection in dialogue with Kwayana, he began to disentangle these politics. He did not quite understand why Brother Eusi always underscored "I am not a politician." But, through his own experience, and his conversations with Eusi Kwayana, Richmond began to see that politicians, preoccupied with electoral and state power, really didn't have working people's interests at heart. Instead politicians used their needs and demands to pose as working people's patron and through this maintained their authority at all costs. A radical democratic or socialist activist had to move beyond concerns with "corruption" as such. That is hierarchical government would always be compromised, and would never regulate corruption. Working people needed to, through their own self-organization, begin to understand the power they held independently.[13]

Democracy, like struggles for national liberation, has two contradictory meanings: the justification of existing and aspiring states and ruling elites versus a tradition of revolutionary popular

---

13   Frank Richmond, interviewed by the author: Spring 2012

liberation, or direct self-government. It was these lessons that were learned in Guyana during the second half of the 20th century, as recognized by Eusi Kwayana and as recorded in *The Bauxite Strike and the Old Politics.*

Dedicated to the working people of

Guyana, and especially of Linden.

"The sayings of the poor are not quoted."
— Akan Proverb

"Every cook must learn to govern."
— Lenin

" 'tone deh battam ribbah, 'e na know 'ow sun 'at."
— Guyanese proverb

The Bauxite Strike and the Old Politics

By Eusi Kwayana

Why this Book is Written

It was CLR James who, to my knowledge, first outlined, and developed to some point, the special role of political parties in the developing countries, especially among transplanted peoples. He saw them not only as agents of mobilization and education or reconstruction but as a new public moral authority of the people. Not many of the parties have proved equal to the task.

This book describes the plight of the old politics in the new times. One after the other, many promising political parties have packed up as people's parties to become leaders' parties. In James's *Party Politics in the West Indies* (1962) we read:

> Mr. Manley, Sir. Grantley Adams, Dr. Williams, Dr. Jagan are all men of very different personalities. But the political personality of each is today cast in the same mold. They are more like one another than they are like anybody else. Watch this [sic].

By now other names may be added to the list.

One of the serious weaknesses of the political culture of the West Indies is that, more than in any other place, with the exception of Africa, politics has become the chief means of upward mobility or social promotion. It is a step to what people consider "success," "eminence," "distinguishedness," and so on. For this reason, in the West Indies, anyone who dares to question a political action, or even discuss it, is at once accused by the circle of political assistants and climbers of wanting to undermine, or take over the Prime Minister's "leadership" or position. And often the charge is correct. Then a high percentage of the population think that taking over political power is the only proper thing to do in the present conditions. All of this shows a state of political culture in which rulers show little humanity and people lose their high ideals and faith in a decent future. Leaders do not see the relationship between political leadership and leadership in general. While it is true that political leadership can often be the overall inspirer and coordinator, political leadership itself will be most successful where other healthy areas of leadership are free to flourish.

Our Caribbean people must be encouraged to develop all kinds of leadership, learn that people can distinguish themselves and be extremely useful citizens at building, at politics, at agriculture, at artistic work, at typing, at science, religion at business organization and so on. A Prime Minister, in the absence of a proper party organization and political system, becomes the man in whom everyone has hope. Up to that point, the prime-minister-culture is quite good. To have a man who has his eyes on the ball in this new life of independence is good for us. But hope can move over into its opposite.

Our aim should be to help him and the organization in the big work to be done. This help does not mean only obedience. Obedience will often be necessary. But to help only by obedience is really not to help, but to flatter; and flattery is the worst food for a political leader. The kind of help a political leader needs—and often does not know his needs—is assistance in developing an ideology which can be taught seriously to the people, help in motivating and strengthening the people; friendly, private criticism; when that fails, open criticism of the regime; and help in the creation of a new order of public morality in which everyone has confidence. HH Nicholson wanted to render such help, but the P.M. would not hear of it when proposed.

I have been referred to in the past as the Prime Minister's adviser. I have never been appointed to any such post. Whenever the Prime Minister felt he wanted advice from me he got it, frank and free. Whenever I thought the Prime Minister needed the kind of advice I could give, I gave it, frankly and freely, without money and without price. As the slander develops I shall have to say more on this point. I have seen in a newspaper a claim that I even attended cabinet meetings. I have never attended cabinet meetings. As Chairman of a committee to investigate changing of the Guyana Coop Credit Society into a Coop Bank and as a Chairman of a Cooperative Insurance Committee I was, along with other committee members, present at those items on the agenda to explain the reports to the Cabinet. As Chairman of Guyana Marketing Corporation, I once attended an Economic Sub-Committee of the Cabinet to discuss and receive directives on GMC capital estimates. I do not see why a political reporter should have me "attending cabinet meetings."

My own view is that while the system lasts, Prime Ministers and Political Leaders should only rarely be subject to change, throwing out, and putting in. Their term of office should be as long as possible. The office should not be regarded as a juicy plum. For ex-colonial people, and for black people, if the leaders are trying to carry out an anti-colonial people's revolution, they should be supported. But, in turn, they must guarantee their comrades and their countrymen that they will rule by some healthy set of principles; that if there is any discrimination in the law it will be in favor of the weak and against the strong; that they will not permit at any level, through jealousy or narrow mindedness, talents and abilities to be suppressed; that they will give their people an ideology and have it developed by lively criticism and discussion, so that if for some reason they are not on the spot or no longer available, the party, its organs and the people will be able to carry on. In a country founded on African slavery, the descendants of these slaves must be specially aided to overcome disabilities due to history.

A party that cannot stand up to mild criticism, and benefit from it, is blowing short. A party that is in the government and cannot accept and offer moral challenges is in a state of decay. Of many parties in the West Indies, it can be said "leaf fall a'wata; e na a-ratten same time."

Parties which cannot respond to healthy opinions, parties which protect those who offend the people from the wrath of the people; Parties which suppress their healthy elements are falling into a nice little trap.

Any Party which is serious can hold a special conference at any time and deal with its internal weaknesses, purge itself, make itself battle worthy, and live on. This does not play into the hands of the opposition, but upsets the opposition. Not to do it plays into the hands of the opposition.

It is possible that, because this is being written in Guyana, what is said about political parties will be believed to refer only to Guyana and then only to the People's National Congress, the governing party. This is not so. The PNC is trying hard to distinguish itself from other Caribbean parties. It is different in some positive ways. It is similar in many negative ways. It is the same in the conception of leadership. Like the others it has launched an attack on the black organization. Many people will think that these things do not apply to the People's Progressive Party. That is where they are wrong.

The PPP led by Cheddi Jagan, in the 22 years of its existence has not put forward a single new idea. It has based its political support since 1956 on East Indians. It wants to be known abroad as a socialist party, but all Guyanese know it is an Indian party. It leads the ethnic group with the largest native bourgeoisie or capitalist class. Throughout its history therefore it could not escape the total gravitational pull of the Indian community, the bourgeoisie included.

Many do not know that the PPP declared, very seriously on three occasions, that it would not nationalize the bauxite industry and the sugar industry. It is now claiming that this was a matter of tactics. It was indeed—the tactics of opportunism. On the first occasion, Jagan was attempting to forge links with British capitalism. It was the occasion of the visit of the Rootes Mission, and the "socialist" Jagan as chief minister in his government made this joint declaration with the imperialist mission. The second time, Jagan made this statement was in 1961 before the National Press Club (USA) in Washington D.C. when he had gone to the USA to fraternize with Kennedy and seek the alliance of the "liberal" wing of US Imperialism. The third time, he made this statement was in the PPP's 1964 election manifesto. Here he gave reasoned arguments to explain why his mixed economy did not need to nationalize bauxite and sugar.

The PPP, following the split in 1955 when the urban workers parted company with it, won the support of the British government after defeating the Burnham Party by means of a racist election campaign in 1957. The British government assisted the "feared" PPP to hold power by allowing Jagan to nominate members to Parliament so that he could have a majority to control the government. For seven years, the PPP functioned thus with the support of Anglo-US Imperialism. So comfortable was Jagan that in the 1960's he proposed an "independence" constitution that offered to leave foreign affairs and defense in British hands. After the PPP won the 1961 election Sir Jock Campbell, now Lord of Somewhere, said "Dr. Jagan and I get on very well, despite his ideology." Between 1961 and 1964, this supposedly revolutionary party deepened the contradictions between African and Indian by calling British troops to assist the Government in its deliberate confrontation, organized by itself, with rural African workers and farmers. Jagan is fond of quoting *A Thousand Days* against Burnham. The essence of what Schlesinger wrote is that the British preferred Jagan to Burnham while the Americans preferred Burnham to Jagan for their own purposes. But even the White House regarded him as a woolly ideologist. The Yankee writer was interested in using people.

In the ideological field the PPP, far from developing any social-ist theory with relevance to Guyana, became the official mouth-piece of Moscow's foreign policy. It accepted (on our behalf) the doctrine of limited sovereignty, which can be very bad encour-agement for the USA. Jagan signed the Moscow declaration in regard to Czechoslovakia and attacked the Chinese Party...(As I said at a YSM Seminar at Madwini, the great contribution of the PNC was to change Guyana's outlook from outward to inward and open the way for the development of an ideology. I added that the PNC had not yet developed that ideology.) The PPP has failed to raise the peasant question.

The Africans throughout the colonial period were deprived of any compensation. The PPP has not been able to deal with this historical plunder of the African people and thus cannot pretend to have a relevant ideology. Jagan has not advanced beyond the Puerto Rico "500 acre law." To face the peasant question is also to face the question of Indian plantation owners in their semi-feudal relationship with Indian peasants, who by and large, from top to bottom, are all PPP supporters.

So much for political parties. All organizations develop vested interests. Then the people in the leadership also develop vested interests. The "White lady" general secretary of the PPP[1] in 1953 on election victory night described the party PPP as her "baby" at a mass victory rally. The world press regards her as "Marxist."

The vested interests of organizations, whatever they call themselves, must be carefully observed. They may range from positive to negative, from liberation to re-enslavement, from good works to banditry. As there is no true criticism without self criticism, here is a word about ASCRIA.

We have a vested interest in black people. When we criticize others it is not to claim that we are without faults, but we are free

1   Refering to Janet Rosenberg Jagan, Cheddi Jagan's Chicago-born wife, who later became president of Guyana from 1997-1999. -ed.

from power and therefore are in a liberated position. This leaves us free to see. Our vested interest in black people can reach the point of a fault. For example, from discussion in the organization, it is clear that many feel I myself have a vested interest in unity and that I may advise unity at too high a price. Criticism helps the mind of individuals and the mind of organizations to grow.

A serious obstacle to growth in many organizations is the power complex. When an individual develops a vested interest in office or in power, it is finished. Every suitable process and device must be used. Power should be decentralized and made collective. Subordinate bodies must time and again be entrusted with higher functions. If man is a sincere builder, we should be fully occupied with this problem for the remainder of this century. "Every cook must learn to govern," as Lenin said.

This tract is being written because we need a careful record of the events during the bauxite strike which took place between the decision to nationalize DEMBA and vesting day. It is being written to expose the whispering campaigns which surrounded the events.

The main report was completed about June /July 1971. Only now is it possible for the book to be produced.

Many events have taken place since the main part of the tract was completed. Since then ASCRIA has been accused of wanting to undermine and overthrow the government of independent Guyana. PNC members have been ordered not to associate with ASCRIA. But this book is not about such recent developments.

Chapter One:
Breakdown

The April events at Linden the bauxite town in Guyana, the former Mackenzie City, are such as do not happen very often in the history of a society. It was lucky for Guyana that they happened. If the right lessons are drawn from them, we can avoid more profound upheavals in the future. The revolt of the workers was directed in actual fact against four institutions of the old society:

1) the old Trade Union system
2) the old political system
3) the old system of leadership, and...
4) the old communications system, which was the hand maiden of the other three.

What shows more than anything else, the bankruptcy of the Trade Union practice, was the fact that the men who emerged as strike leaders and leaders of the mass action were the very men expelled by the Union in August 1970;[1] an act taken by the union to prevent the brothers from contesting union elections. Okomofo (Desmond Moffat) and Kwame (Martin Bobb) are not upstarts or demagogues who suddenly tricked their way into popular favor, but comrades who had long been connected with the shop floor struggles of the workers for improvements and for the recognition by the leaders of the existence of the union membership.

The Trade Union leadership thinks of itself as, and sets out to be, a bureaucracy. This can be understood, even though we think it is a wrong conception. The company, DEMBA, keeps its

---

1   Martin Bobb, Macintosh and Quamina were expelled by the Union executive. Odida Huntley was suspended for one year.

head office in Georgetown. This is perhaps because Georgetown is the port, the administrative and political hub of things. Another compelling reason for their Georgetown Headquarters would be that in the past, communications with Mackenzie were very bad. They are still poor. The recently built highway (1965) has to some degree improved the physical communications between DEMBA and the city by ending the limited passenger and goods traffic by steamer to Mackenzie-Wismar-Christianburg, now Linden. DEMBA was also mainly concerned with keeping its pulse on the Guyanese society. Its public relations men were in the past very active socially. They tried to charm middle class groups and to capture the minds of our bright young men and women. Another reason for an impressive Georgetown presence was the need for the leaders of DEMBA to be in direct touch with other Europeans in Guyana, so as to be able to identify their areas of rivalry, their contradictions, and their lines of neocolonialist conspiracy against the Guyanese people and their government.

What led the union to set up headquarters in Georgetown is not clear, it might at one time have thought this necessary as a means of matching company propaganda in the city. Another reason might be the reduction of the expenses of large delegations coming to Georgetown for annual negotiations. This initiative, which might at first have been aimed at savings for the union, contained in it a Georgetown fixation which later on led to waste instead of savings. The Headquarters in Hadfield Street soon became too humble for the Union delegates who had to match the DEMBA bureaucracy in order to uphold what is called "image" or at times "status," allegedly so as to be respected by the bosses.

The Guyana Mine Workers Union (GMWU) has, for many years, had problems centered on the Union Bureaucracy. To the casual observer, it seemed that leaders were chosen and idolized by a supposedly fickle membership, only to be dethroned later on when tastes changed. Many union leaders or other leaders elected by the people also carry this crippling insecurity in their minds, an insecurity which makes them compromise with principle. The popular leaders of this kind usually are without a revolutionary ideology so that they see themselves as " leaders" or as men whose positions are based on their brilliance, ability, and charm. It is not for nothing that western writers place so much stress on "charisma" among leaders but only in the non-white world. One seldom hears of "charisma" among the whites of Britain, or France, or USA or USSR. The leaders do not see the struggle as a dynamic process of forces against forces. They exaggerate the role of the individual leaders and underrate the role of consciousness among the people. So too, the union leaders did not see themselves as part of a dynamic movement. They were moved by their basic sense of insecurity to shift the priorities from representation of the people to self-compensation. Things came to such a pass that, at the time of the April strike, the three leading officers of the union were all resident outside of the bauxite belt, in greater Georgetown.

The isolation of the union's leadership was a consequence of its concept of its own work and of its relationship to the union membership. This isolation was long developing. In many engagements with the power structure in Linden, the official union view seemed to have been one of ready compromise. This view did not at all reflect the opinion of the large body of workers. Most of the DEMBA workers, at all levels, seem to posses the skill of analyzing very carefully the slightest act, statement, or proposal of the management. No group of workers understand their work situation so well as the bauxite workers of Guyana. Their intelligence is sharpened by their job experience, by their various victories and disappointments and perhaps by the fact that they have, until recently been bound to live in the most stratified community in Guyana, with its South African and American idea of neighborhood living and of white supremacy. The physical arrangements of the industry were such also that the whole imperialist machinery could be clearly seen; the extraction of the ore, the processing and added value, the shipping away of wealth, the importation of raw chemicals, the small group of expatriate decision makers, the tokenism, the social gaps, the misery of the poorer districts, the hill top luxury of the white population, the buying out of leaders, the divide and rule tactics, the process of exploitation which they could feel in their skin. All of these experiences sharpened the bauxite workers and made them very critical thinkers. In addition, it made them ready for revolutionary theory and revolutionary action.

In 1970, the workers went on strike after a white company official had been found in his shorts prowling, after midnight, in the nurses' hostel. The workers came out on a spontaneous strike, demanding disciplinary measures against the violator of the nursing trainees' peace and privacy. The local Guyana Police Force units turned the man over to the DEMBA's Security Force Units, The company "dismissed" the man who immediately left the country and thus escaped prosecution. So far the political government of the PNC took up a strong stand in favor of the protestors. The Guyana Mine Workers' Union was caught on the hop and was forced to adopt the unofficial strike which the workers had started. The Union leadership saw from the start that the workers' movement was not waiting on it for inspiration. Leadership at the rank and file level was, not for the first time, but with tremendous significance, an important, and, to the leadership, a frightening factor in the situation, a campaign began against the militants.

Always finding it easier to call names, the press labeled the agitators as ASCRIA. Of course, ASCRIA played an important part in the events; but the popular forces in the lead contained other more purely industrial elements, which were free to act without ASCRIA's self-imposed constraints. These elements, again in 1971, were to make the final exposure of traditional trade unionism in a country with a revolutionary mentality and with revolutionary aspirations. GMWU went to work with energy to smear ASCRIA. The company (DEMBA) issued daily bulletins, all tending to attack this "dissident group" of militants who were preventing workers from returning to work. The PPP *Mirror* played a very active part in this anti-ASCRIA campaign. It reported one day that the workers were willing to return to work but were being threatened by young men "with beards."

The workers had gone on strike on Monday. By Thursday, there was a trickle back to work. The issue which was now the cause of tension between the militants and the union leadership was the demand that the physician in charge of the hospital and a sergeant be suspended until the inquiry was over. It was clear at this time that the whole propaganda effort was being directed by DEMBA. It was an issue involving the dignity of black women and it was understandable that the whites should try to obscure the exposure of a white man and to confuse the issues. The *Mirror,* by a long way, outdid the capitalist newspapers in the anti-black slander. It reported that the senior staff were packing up to leave DEMBA "for fear of their lives."

Another area of tension developed later. It was that between the government and the strikers. The official PNC, leadership both at the center and at the local level was, naturally, taking the government's point of view. The ministry did not support the idea of suspending the Medical Superintendent and concentrated its efforts on the idea of an inquiry.

The upshot of the whole episode was that the Union leadership, with President Verbeke in the saddle, came down heavily on the militants and expelled them from the Union. Another of the militants was suspended.

The was not the first time that President Verbeke had been moved to clamp down on a militant wing of the Dade Union. In 1958, a situation had arisen in which the President of the Industrial Branch, Caesar, and his colleagues, including Aaron, the present

MP, were challenging the leadership on the question of expenditure of union funds and alleged tampering with union elections in the Kwakwani area. At an executive meeting which was boycotted by all the militants except Aaron, the idea of expelling Caesar was considered. The president vacillated as Aaron led the attack and demanded that some charge or accusation be laid against Caesar who should be given the right to explain his position or defend himself. A delegate from the interior then declared that they were not there to "listen to sentiment." As a result, Caesar was expelled from the Union.

The matter reached the Supreme Court and much of the issue is recorded in a judgment by Mr. Justice Fraser. The judgment found in Guyana Law Reports does not record the part played by Aaron. However, the Court condemned the action of the Union executive in expelling Caesar.

In 1970, the ASCRIA Compound at Wismar was completely displeased with the performance of the Union executives. They did not hide this feeling. The majority of workers at DEMBA felt the same way. DEMBA's espionage agents were warning the Union leadership of a possible "takeover" by ASCRIA at the next elections of the Union. The entire white community of Guyana seemed to be taking an interest in the possibility of this 'take over' of the union leadership by ASCRIA members and other militants. The expulsions were aimed at preventing this. They would in fact have been futile. Apart from the suspended and expelled individuals, there would be scores of other young workers who could set up a collective community of work and ideas that is usually described as leadership and who could inject dynamism into the union.

The interest of the government, as will be shown later, was in reducing workers' militancy, though the revolutionary elements recognized it as a necessary force for the economic revolution. The government believed that with itself in office and potentially in power, prolonged workers' strikes were unnecessary. The Union leadership knew this, but used it as a means of strengthening its own position with the workers and took no pains to give to government due credit for what it did. The government's strong stand on these matters was therefore known to the ministers concerned, or to the cabinet, the company officials and the Union leadership. No credit went to the party. Workers might even feel that the company was being very flexible. The government claimed that it had always in disputes about wages taken the side of the workers. So, it felt its confidence challenged by those who tried to employ militancy in the place of government power. The fact that the workers did not know what the Prime Minister did positively on their side, and were not aware of the means directed by the government to settle these disputes, was not considered important by the government or the party machinery. The workers were supposed to know somehow; and if they did not know, it was simply a matter of their own neglect. This old method of communication is another of the old institutions overthrown by the workers' April revolt. It will be examined more closely later on.

Because the party machinery at Linden carried out the government's method of communication, a degree of tension grew up between the PNC and ASCRIA at Linden (August 1970)—tension that was a result of an industrial situation and levels of consciousness in responding to that situation, and not a result of questions of central government leadership or authority. The PPP made a great deal of play of this local tension and printed such headlines as "showdown between PNC and ASCRIA."

The Wismar Compound of ASCRIA knew that the Union leadership was bankrupt, and individual members on the basis of their relationship with the fellow workers were attempting to fill the gap and not leave the workers disorganized. But as the tension mounted, motives became clouded. People began to use the situation to divide the community by talking of ASCRIA's ambitions of dominating the whole area and eventually, who knows, other areas. So as to clear the air, or rather to give the air time to clear, the Wismar ASCRIA compound was advised by the Council of Elders that its leaders should stand down from union elections and take no active part in them. They did not contest the elections; and for a time, many thought that because of this, society had been saved. The April events must have put an end to any such misjudgments.

One other event must be recounted briefly if a true picture of our involvement must be drawn. It is the issue of the black Guyanese geologist, Owen Young. He was a graduate of a Canadian University and returned to Guyana in DEMBA's employment. His wife was a black woman, born in Canada. Young's tenure at DEMBA was rather brief. The white management maneuvered a confrontation with him and his wife, who did not conceal her resentment of white Canadian contempt. Eventually, Owen Young was dismissed for inefficiency, an issue raised only at the time of dismissal. ASCRIA became deeply involved in the protest and sent a team to the area to hold a public protest meeting, At this meeting, it was decided to appeal on the spot to the workers, for a 24 hours' protest strike. The immediate response of the workers, who had probably put the suggestion to Kwame Apata, the main speaker, closed down operations for the next 24 hours. After internal disputes about how long the strike should go, it was ended with good discipline at the end of the period set. This independent action of the part of the workers frightened the union executive, the PNC and most of all the company.[2] They both concluded that it needed an outside force to come and "cause" a strike. One

---

[2] The Government did not like ASCRIA's involvement in the affair. It was probably of the opinion that the Youngs were, on the whole, a tactless couple. However, the Ministry of Labor gave practical support at the time when payments due to Owen Young by the company were being negotiated.

of the main reasons why this pamphlet is being written is to let the people of Guyana and especially PNC supporters, who know least about this area, understand the great and dynamic potential for both positive reconstruction and negative roles lying in the possession of the Linden labor force. It is a kind of public appeal to those mainly concerned to reorganize along revolutionary lines in the area so that precious human resources are not wasted. Since the workers there understand their work situation better than anyone else, it is not possible for outsiders to get them to strike for objectives not connected with that situation.

If we consider together the workers' action in 1968, 1970, and in 1971, and also some of the events of 1958-1959, we cannot escape the view that for many years the Guyana Mineworkers Union has been ineffective, failing to provide leadership for the workers, failing even to make the industrial responses necessary in their situation. The white Canadian personnel spies understood the psychology of the labour force much better than the majority of higher union leaders care to do. We find, then, that on important occasions, the workers have acted without reference to the union, both in their response to the white supremacist attitude and on industrial matters which in their opinion required militancy. Cedric Grant shows how DEMBA attempted to fashion the GMWU in its own image and likeness. Dealing with the period after the great Mackenzie strike of 1947, Cedric Grant points out :

> Once it ceased to oppose unionism, the Company strove, for example, to fashion the Guyana Mine Workers' Union into its North American image. North American unionists came on the Mackenzie scene as part of their own program to contain the internationally integrated aluminum industry and to standardize its condition of employment. They taught patterns of labor-management relations

that fitted in with the industrial context created by DEMBA, and that worked well enough in going through the motions of the day-to-day resolution of minor industrial differences. [sic]

More often than not results of the industrial relationship were exactly the reverse of the intentions of the Company. For one thing the trade union legislation in Guyana was British oriented. For another, the bauxite trade unionists had either served as leaders in the oldest trade union, the Guyana Labour Union, in Guyana (and the Commonwealth Caribbean) or were inspired by its militancy particularly among the dockworkers in Georgetown. In consequence, as DEMBA put it, the GMWU tended to throw aside these North American methods of bargaining 'in the face of sudden emotional crisis in the Mackenzie community, and the union leader who emerged was the strong voice raised in eloquent but not necessarily constructive protest at the head of a marching group of demonstrating workers.' That Mackenzie has developed into a crisis ridden community is not surprising, since the North American trade unionists were not particularly concerned or conversant with the industrial experiences of the trade unionists in an essentially sugar plantation society. (From: Cedric Grant, *Company Towns In The Caribbean*, 14-15)

If we accept this quoted confession of Rosane, an expatriate DEMBA official and propagandist, it throws some light on why the union leadership soon became separated in temper from the general work force. The North American education succeeded with the leadership, but did not touch the workers, except to call forth from them a sense of self-reliance.

These are interesting aspects of trade union development. The test that must be applied to answer why the union failed, especially at this time, should be one of class alignment, one of ideology and one of methods, all of which are inter-related.

In terms of class, the official leaders of the union soon lost working class tastes and working class feeling. What has stuck in the head, by their trips to the USA and their contact with capitalistic unions, is that they must develop a bureaucracy to match that of the employers. In a trade union, however, bureaucracy is more explosive than in most other associations. It works roughly this way: There is an election which is fought with or without energy, depending on the interest of the members and the general internal situation of the union. This election is expected to settle for another year or so the question of where "leadership" is to come from. In the case of the GMWU, the principal officers then sail away from the base, Linden, if they were there at the time of election, to their new found places of residence—usually Georgetown. There, they are used as sounding boards by the company, for company policy. The leadership becomes isolated from the industrial politics of the company town. The only connection between them and the workforce is their view of the workers as mere wage slaves, and that they expect the workers to have no other concerns but wages.

This is the old unionism that crashed in April. It was objectively the main target of the workers' revolt. To rebuild the same structure with new people will merely discredit these new people or put them under unreasonable strain. Fortunately, the new leadership does not *at first* present the problem in the form of who is to be president, or secretary or treasurer. It poses the question of how the machinery is to be organized and what should be its objectives. These solutions must allow for the widespread democratic distribution of initiative and talents. The union executive that is constituted on the basis of a parliament will find that it lacks the reflexes to deal with an industrial situation. The old style union leadership saw itself as reacting to company measures and company initiatives. Hence, the company was continually choosing the battleground and deciding, so to speak, on the areas of war. Even under imperialism, the workers are entitled to expect more of their union. But typical trade union politics sees the unions as bargainers over "the terms on which labor power is to be sold." In the context of nationalization, the union should have been able to forecast the new system. But since the leadership had become a new stratum and no longer identified with the workers, it failed to see things from their point of view.

Without any attempt at phrase-mongering, it must be said that a socialist society cannot be served with bourgeois or capitalist conceived trade unions. The unions, by their nature, conceive the workers as wage slaves and because of this see them as having so much authority so much responsibility and no more. Imagine their terror when for 15 days they had to look on helplessly while the workers conducted their own affairs! What was even more remarkable was the fact that both those who supported the strike, and the other group who for tactical nationalist reasons, did not support it, as well as those who organized the continuation of work, were acting and carrying on their affairs without the help of the union executive. The bureaucrats had completely lost currency not only with the labor force but with the population at Linden. It was the decay of the old unionism and the birth of the new. It is the law of history that the new is born before the old is dead and moreover that it is out of contradiction and conflict in the body of the old organization that the germ of the new one is conceived. This is exactly what happened.

No one can say at this moment what the new trade unionism will be like in a revolutionized economy. Should the workers spend effort in rebuilding an organ which became necessary because of capitalism? Can the workers, along with their political party, design a new organ of workers' self-expression and workers' power? Can we work out a method by which workers at all levels are represented in the decision making bodies, and which can carry the mood of the worker into management organs? If all this can be written into the new design, what will be the role of the Unions?

Socialist countries have a ready-made pattern of what trade unions do after nationalization, but this may not be the answer we seek. Will it be a crime against Guyanese or Caribbean democracy if a new strategy is developed giving more authority to the workers than they enjoy in present unions, supplementing collective bargaining with collective planning and collective decision making? It is too early in the history of industrialization for workers to give up the idea of trade unions, which in the last resort can go into battle for the class. Workers, especially if they do not know what the system really is, and suspect all political changes, will correctly want to keep their union as an instrument under their absolute control. All of these fears result from the degree of alienation which imperialism has imposed among us, and which capitalism always imposes wherever it gets going and which, some argue, takes place wherever technology has become important. This alienation is often sharpened by the conduct of the new political, managerial and trade union elite. Whatever solutions are developed or attempted, it is important to note that the April revolt has warned against the development of a new, closed bureaucracy and has shown clearly that there are great resources of talent, service and leadership among the rank and file workers. The new management will have to find a way of employing these talents and helping them to find expression. As for the present union executive, its authority with the workers can be seen from the fact that the workers expelled by it less than a year ago have now driven it into a corner by mass action.

Chapter Two:
The Setting

An examination of the role of the government in the April revolt is very, very important, since people are entitled to make judgments on the basis of events. The importation of the opposition in the dispute is another matter of wide interest, especially internationally.

Like the party headquarters, the government was taken by surprise when the strike broke out. A gloomy mood of disappointment settled over it. From the start, the Ministry of Labor paralyzed itself by holding on to some basic principle that workers must first return to work before solutions could be attempted. In general, the government tended to be shocked at the apparent thoughtlessness of the striking workers. It was also fully aware that the strike could work havoc with nationalization. Nevertheless, it tended to regard the labor dispute as an ordinary strike, and stuck to its normal procedures. Its difficulties were increased by the fact that the strike was an unofficial one, and that the union could not speak for the strikers. When the Minister of Labor visited the scene of the dispute on April 20, the contradictions between the strikers and the government were brought very clearly into focus. The air was full of words of defiance and accusations that involved the government. They said that frauds were taking place in most government departments; that the External Trade Bureau had failed and that anything the government put its hand to failed.

The whole confusion was brought out very clearly by the Prime Minister when some weeks after he said to a group of DEMBA workers: You have a dispute with your union, why bring the government into it? So far as the workers were concerned, the union was nothing but a tool of the party and of the government.

They accused the union of being run from Congress Place. They recalled the support given by the party organization in Mackenzie, in 1970, to the election of the union leadership's candidates when the bulk of the labor force had long lost confidence in the leadership. Workers are not likely to forget these big historical incidents in their life, but in a busy party organization, the incident may be seen as nothing more than one directive among many directives.

The government had further involved itself in the dispute by the support it gave to the workers through the union. One worker even hinted that nationalization would fail, like the External Trade Bureau and Global Agriculture, and referred to the corporate union investigation, and the prosecution of an employee of Guyana Marketing Corporation. All these things had formulated in the mind of the workers as reasons why the civil servants could not be trusted with money. They had been brought to feel rather strongly that, if vesting day came before the arbitration award, the money due to workers would be "confiscated" by government—a line ALCAN has been using in its anti-nationalization campaign. Thus, the workers, who had supported nationalization politically and who for other reasons would have wanted a swift take-over, now saw their economic interests as being in contradiction with a swift take-over.

The record shows that it was never any part of the government's plan to "confiscate" either DEMBA's assets (i.e. without compensation) or workers' benefits. The Prime Minister had stated, prior to the strike, that the arbitration award would be retroactive to February 1970. The fact that a vibrant section of the labor force could be made to believe that the government, its own government would seize workers' earnings and entitlements can be accounted for only in one or two ways. One possibility was that absence of communication, absence of party organization, and lack of contact with the leadership had left the workers entirely without information about their industrial future. While this is generally true, it is not likely that DEMBA workers did not know that the Prime Minister himself had given an undertaking about the Tyndall arbitration award. The workers at Linden are generally well documented, not only in their own affairs but on all political affairs. It seems then that they did not accept, or no longer accepted, this undertaking. Why? They no longer accepted this undertaking which they had seemed to in February, when the Prime Minister addressed them at Wismar and Mackenzie.

The change resulted from the subtle propaganda of the Company, ALCAN's DEMBA. They did not have to reject government. They needed only to doubt it. ALCAN provided the raw material—hostile but subtle "rational " propaganda for these doubts. As the company was a party in the arbitration, it had some sense of the thoroughness with which Mr. Tyndall, chairman, and his tribunal were going into the question of the arbitration. It also knew that the union had not completed its presentation and perhaps also the reasons why. The situation at DEMBA was such that the management had many opportunities for passing on their propaganda to the workers. Staff conferences with the Guyanese management, briefings with the foremen and general foremen, a fortnightly newspaper, a word dropped in the right ear, statements by the Canadian manager in Guyana, statements by ALCAN and the various methods used after the crisis left just the kind of climate DEMBA wanted to suit its purposes. DEMBA did not care whether the workers believed, or even understood its line of propaganda. What was important was to create doubts in their minds. With a working class doubting its leaders, a counter revolution has all it can desire.

The more immediate leadership of the workers is industrial, in which area it is expected that the trade union will take care of their needs. The failure of the Guyana Mine Workers' Union to keep the confidence of the workers was the chief motivating force of the April events. The union had become a bureaucracy and a very inefficient one at that. How remote the trade union leaders were from their members is shown by the fact that not one of the three leading officers lived in the Bauxite Belt, but in Georgetown. At Mackenzie, DEMBA's falsifiers were always present.

The other plane of leadership to which the workers could look was their party, the People's National Congress. The party in the bauxite area, and the leadership in the city, showed no sign of any plan for reorganization in a revolutionary situation. At one sweep, the government, which had taken the boldest step since the Berbice Revolution in 1763 by nationalizing DEMBA, was being seriously questioned by the workers, who took to the streets in a trade union dispute, denouncing the party and the government, but being rather quiet about the rich instigator, DEMBA.

There was no disagreement between the government and ourselves about the principle of nationalization, the principle cooperative development, and the ownership and control of resources by non-exploitative groups of people. ASCRIA, however, believes that nationalization without workers' control and workers' self-management is a fraud. And there is every lack of agreement on the role of the party and the party's responsibilities, even now that there is an intensification of party energy all over the country.

Linden is a clear example of the response of industrial workers to a line of political inaction in the moment of profound change. At one sweep, the party and the government had cut down the old authority at DEMBA, without being able to put anything in its place. In place of the old authority we had the DEMBA officials themselves, occupying their accustomed positions until vesting day. There were the white officials from ALCAN headquarters continuing to pass down instructions, and, from the point of view of the workers, remaining in a position from which they could sabotage the enterprise. Even a number of Guyanese managers were uneasy at these arrangements. They all knew what harm could be done by the giving of wrong instructions between the passing of the Nationalization Act and Vesting Day itself. They did not trust the members of the company's old guard who had suddenly swung over to the side of the people. The period also showed the impossibility of successfully managing a socialized enterprise, with a capitalistic machine or something worse than that. Again, we ourselves feel that nationalization without workers control is a fraud. The workers expected to be given information about their future and to be involved in the planning, but nothing like this happened and the workers sought means of making their displeasure known. Whatever reasons were given by the strikers for the strike, it was, objectively, the response of those workers with the strongest sense of alienation to a moment of historical and social change that affected their lives, seeing that their future roles had not been clearly defined.

It has been shown that the public declarations of the Prime Minister about job security and about the arbitration award were very clear. These are again provided for in the Bauxite Nationalization Act 1971.

> In so far as they relate to assets and liabilities of the Company which become assets and liabilities of the State by virtue of this Act, all contracts, deeds, bonds, agreements and other instruments of whatever nature subsisting or affecting the Company shall, subject to the provisions of any law imposing limitations on the liability of the State, be of full force and effect against or in favor of the State as if in the place of the Company the State had been named therein or had been a party thereto and where immovable property has, by virtue of this Act, vested in the State the Registrar of Deeds shall

> take due notice thereof and shall make such anno-
> tations on the records as may be necessary.

An important problem of this examination is to determine why, in spite of all this, a group of the workers at DEMBA did not accept the assurance given to them about their future. We are still to learn to understand what happens inside human beings who are forced to live and perform on a scale below their potential; but this can be a serious problem of human oppression which only society as a whole can solve. One possible explanation for the loss of confidence in a situation like this can be imperialist provoca-tion. Some members of the government and party expressed this opinion. It was bolstered by the fact that, since $5 million had al-legedly been offered to the Prime Minister by a company official to "use as he pleased," this $5 million was available for provocation and corruption. While some workers showed an ugly mood, no evidence has been produced of the circulation or distribution of large sums of money. Moreover those who have personal knowl-edge of Moffat consider him incorruptible and those who know Bobb do not think he will accept money from imperialists for such purposes. The government has still to explain why no action has been taken. What is there to gain politically by hiding the facts from the country?

The Minister of Labor, on April 19, scored a success with the workers although he himself did not recognize it. After doing battle with several extremely hostile groups of workers, the Min-ister was advised by workers, through the Coordinating Elder of ASCRIA, to address the workers and put forward a solution. The ASCRIA representative had been greeted with a long stream of attacks from the workers: it was purely a union matter and no interference was wanted; this was not ASCRIA; ASCRIA supports the government; this was the only direct attack on the organiza-tion. When the Elder replied "Yes, ASCRIA supports the government," there was no follow up except "We have respect for you, so keep out of out this; matter gone far." Above all, the Coordinating Elder was asked by voices in the crowd not to speak to the workers, as they were not prepared to hear him. He replied that he wanted to listen to them since they were in distress. He said that he could not speak to them as he was not up to date with the history of the dispute. He listened to this barracking of the government through him for over an hour and learned a great deal of the grievances of the workers. They were complaining, with much accuracy, that no one in the rest of Guyana thought that they, the DEMBA workers, had any need for money. They considered that no one had any sympathy with them, and it was obvious that this made them bitter. They said that the union was a tool. They said that any other workers could strike and be recognized, but that whenever DEMBA workers went on strike, they were confronted with intensive propaganda about the national economy, and they were represented as bloodthirsty and selfish wreckers of the nation. They claimed that in a labor dispute about wages—the sugar industry at once brings forth all the pressures of the government for a rapid solution; that the bauxite workers never received such prompt attention because everyone thought they could wait. They complained about the age old problem of water supply and the problem of the hospital, claiming they had been fooled by government and were tired of promises. They accused the union of being "directed from Congress Place." They were also threatening that if the Prime Minister did not come at their request, the leader of the opposition would be invited to Linden. Some of the voices uttered definitely anti-nationalization comments such as, "Everything government go in is a failure—look External Trade Bureau, look at Cooperative!" Comments like this show that the strikers did not look sympathetically at the government's attempts at settling long outstanding problems. The workers, through all of this, continued to show exceptional faith in the Prime Minister, and demanded again and again that he should visit the area to give them assurances on the spot. Comments were made about the fact that the stronghold always responded to the political directives of the PNC and its leader and that it was high time now for Burnham to come to them at their request. Mr. Carrington, the Minister of Labour, had gone to Linden with a solution in mind—a solution that in the end proved to be acceptable, in principle, to the workers. The attack from the strikers on any one who arrived was very well organized and very thorough. But all through, the workers were anxious to communicate, even through this hostility, the fact being that what they wanted was money rather than excuses and promises. No solution that did not include the payout of their increased wages could be thought of at all.

The press did not bring out the fact that Carrington, the Minister of Labor had been allowed to address the workers in the Union Hall compound on April 19. When word went around that the Minister had a solution, the strikers broke up their knots and formed a large semi-circle around him as he mounted a box. This was a turn in the situation, surprising to those who had misinterpreted the mood of the workers. However, it sprang out of the desire of the strikers for news about the arbitration award.

Chapter Three:
The Government

On Wednesday, April 29, the government found itself in a state of positive inactivity. The Minister of Labor, who had remained overnight in Linden, had changed his line and was laying more emphasis on the question of the "cheek" of the workers who had given the Prime Minister the ultimatum, than on other aspects. It seems that he had gone back to the position that it was impossible to bring pressure to the arbitration tribunal and was hoping to argue the workers back to work. Thus all the positive effect of his Tuesday's statement was quickly lost. The idea of " mastering" people and getting them to move in a crisis against the current of their convictions was a strongly held principle with the PNC. In the crisis it was the dominant and the only political idea of their active members. The strikers had erred and strayed from their ways like lost sheep and they must restore themselves in the good opinion of the party by calling off the strike and accepting assurances from the established leaders—persons whom they no longer relied on.

On Wednesday April 20, as a supporter of nationalization, I reported to the Prime Minister at Belfield and told him the brutal facts of the situation. "It cannot be uglier then it is at Linden," I reported. I explained the barracking I had received from the workers, who thought I had been sent by the government to speak to them and were anxious to prevent this.[1] I explained to the Prime Minister that although it was impracticable to go to Linden in response to the ultimatum, he should nevertheless go, because that was what the strikers wanted. I advised that they would accept

---

1   I had, on a few occasions since the PNC took over the government, advised workers against the use of the strike weapon.

no other solution. I advised that the tribunal should be made to isolate the monetary award, as Carrington had suggested, and to deal with that. I also advised him that the workers had rejected the idea of a two week period before actual payment of the awards; and I urged him to put pressure on the arbitrator to hurry up. That same day, Mr. Tyndall was reported in the press as saying that the Tribunal could not be pressured. I advised the Prime Minister that having seen the arbitrator, he should announce the solution, and at the same time note that he was "coming up to Linden for a conversation with the workers, not to lecture to them but to listen to their complaints and grievances and to place before them issues facing the Industry." The point was made that such a plan would at once raise the status of the workers and, in actual fact, help them and the government to come to grips with the industrial problem of nationalization.

The Prime Minister had no objection to going up. His only concern was that each time there was a dispute the workers would want Burnham to go and solve it. I replied that people were not likely to think in those terms. He asked whether he was expected to run every ministry in his government.

I replied that he might find that he had to run every crisis as Prime Minister.

When the Prime Minister's announcement came out on Sunday, April 25, it was clear that he had been better advised. The workers did not consider his statement clear, and worst of all, the statement did not include the promise to visit Linden. Why? No doubt because of pressures from the social wing of the PNC, which was against the Prime Minister's "stepping down" and being ordered about by the workers. It was quite a comedy to see them stamping their feet and protesting, "What! He is Prime Minister of this country. Why must he run behind them like some boy...?"

The Prime Minister had no objection to going to Linden, but the social wing—that group which is more social than political, more concerned with prestige than with policy—continued to bleat their mournful protests in his ear. It seems that Dr. Reid, the Deputy Prime Minister, was in a special position. He publicly opposed the Prime Minister's going to Linden at that time, but apparently for different reasons. He does not belong to the social wing.

On April 26, I again saw the Prime Minister and discussed Linden at length. We discussed the various personalities involved and their reasons for being involved. I advised the Prime Minister that if he went to Linden a turn would begin, but that after that the party must work ceaselessly, especially at the whole question of ideology. The argument ran something like this:

> Linden is your main citadel. The industry has been nationalized. You cannot play with such a situation. The industry will need the complete solidarity of the workers there. The workers have lost faith in all the ministers except you. This is what they're saying. They say that the union is a tool of Congress Place, that it takes orders. If they say publicly that a visit and assurance from you will solve everything, then why not go? The PNC people up there will not agree with my recommendation. The ASCRIA compound will not agree; they feel it will give strength to Moffat and Bobb. But, this is a national crisis and we cannot be too concerned with who gets kudos and all of that. There was a labor problem in Poland some time ago. The Communist Party leaders kept themselves away. They did not go down to negotiate with the workers. Indeed, the police were brought into it. So inhuman and insensible were the police that they treated the workers as outcasts. Just when the war weary workers were returning to work, the

police opened fire on them, killing many. "They had to change the Prime Minister," I pointed out and went on, "You can get the workers back by starving them out, and by strong arm methods, but they will go back with bitterness in their hearts against you. You can't afford that. The country can't afford it.

Some people talk about stepping down. What stepping down? It's not white people you going to meet. Is your own people. You can't step down to your own people.

Burnham: I have no problem about stepping down, you know. I don't see it so. But we may be building up a cult of personality. They have a Minister of Labor. How do I know that I would not be setting a precedent by going ... ?

Me: What is the alternative?

The "alternative" was a well known colonial method.

The tragedy was that at that very moment, a PNC team, led by the General Secretary, was in the Linden area to "make an assessment." The men who went up there had no intention of admitting that only Burnham could get the people back to work. They were afraid to admit that only he could give them the necessary assurances from his own mouth. The last thing they wanted to do was to confess their inability to influence the situation. The fact that they should think that the outcome depended on charisma, or on charm, is an indication of their poor understanding of the situation.

The inactivity of the government delegation, which traveled up to Linden and remained there for the purpose of looking around, was curious. It is better to leave aside all gossip, even reliable gossip, and deal only with facts that have a direct bearing on interpretation.

It is my view that Dr. Reid, the Deputy Prime Minister, is a man of great commitment to the nation. His indignation at the strike was due to what he could only see as the placing of smaller issues, like the day when the award should be paid, before broader national (and international) issues, like nationalization. He is basically a peasant philosopher and does not appreciate the temper of the industrial workers. So far as he knew, he was speaking the truth when he said, as reported in the press: "You have made it extremely difficult for the Prime Minister..." After strikers referred to police action on the previous day, Dr. Reid told them that whatever happened at Mackenzie was because of what the strikers had done:

> If your children are gassed, it is because of you. If you are brutalized by the police, it is because of you. Once you are idle all sorts of things will happen. One thing is certain, this government will maintain law and order. It is disgusting as far as I am concerned to see things like this happen. (*Guyana Graphic*, 20th April, 1971)[2]

Dr. Reid had gone to a complex industrial situation with a big peasant's logic and the doctrine of obedience. Since the Party had ordered the workers back to work they should obey the command and not let the party and the Prime Minister down. How far this position can be valid will be discussed in the conclusion. He also undertook that the Prime Minister would go up to Linden when there was a full resumption of work. The General Secretary's, Mr. Green's, activity was rather more obscure. It seems however, that someone had been telling the Prime Minister two things: one, that the situation was rapidly improving and two, that the trou-

---

2   See Appendix, Page 120.

ble was being made by a mere handful of persons. The logic was to get these persons out of the way and to use strong measures against the people.

The Prime Minister had planned to announce on Tuesday April 27, that he would visit Linden on Wednesday April 28, and remain there up to Thursday April 29. His team of "reliable" advisers probably reported to him during Monday night and Tuesday. No announcement was made. The Prime Minister was obviously under pressure for a choice of policy. What followed the lamentably distorted reports he must have received is not known in detail.

The first attempts at arresting the spokesman of the revolt began to take shape on Tuesday night. The police gave the opinion that, if they attempted to arrest people at the Union Hall, a number of persons might be injured, and they did not attempt to arrest anyone.

Okomfo (Moffat) remained at the Union Hall, along with others. The assembled comrades had a strong sense of something going wrong. Kwame felt that it was bound to happen "at any time." About 5 a.m., the union building was surrounded by the Riot Squad (There was no riot there either).

On the south side the soldiers provided a cordon, but took no further part in the action. The police broke a window by means of which they opened the door and entered the building. They announced that they wanted "Moffat and Bobb" at the police station. The strikers wished to know why, but they were told to ask no questions. In number 21 were taken up in the Union Hall. Bobb was kept in the superintendent's room but the others were put in the lock ups. They at first told Bobb that he would be released, but at about 2 a.m. suddenly announced a new line. They explained that because of "new instructions" they would have to charge him. With what? Unlawful assembly. Where? In the Union Hall. He was charged indictably with this offense. The security questioning that went before this was very thinly based. The police wanted to know whether the men had received money from DEMBA.

Later that day, April 27, workers were tear-smoked at the bauxite town and the situation seemed to enter a new stage of consciousness. Information about the shameful brutalizing of people, including children, is still coming in. To our great humiliation, it was a white priest whose appeal to the police to cease their attacks caused them to stop.

It is remarkable that the Prime Minister seems to have been prevented from making his planned announcement on Tuesday for a democratic resolution of the conflict, just in time for the development of incidents in which typical neocolonialist methods were used.

The night of the arrests saw sharp reaction from the workers of Linden, who began to give a real taste of their power. Railway cars used for transportation of bauxite ore were derailed in spite of the heavy security watch.

The police had to deal with a situation which was brought about by the splitting of workers on the issue of the timeliness of the strike and the extent to which they were prepared to accept undertakings. A greater number of workers wanted to work than actually appeared on the job. The strikers, not necessarily working on the decisions of the assembly, had begun to make threats to workers who were seen on their way to work. Others did the rounds making threats to the wives of employees who were at work. The threats were to the effect that wooden houses could be burned. The strike leaders were becoming as desperate as the government. The police attack and arrests increased the prestige of the revolt.

The great mistake made by many people who have had to analyze the situation was to weigh the fact of the number of persons who wanted to turn out to work as an important factor in deciding the trend of events. This was a mistake. Social power and ability to decide what happened were in the hands of the revolt.

As pointed out very early, one of the significant achievements of the revolt was the overthrow of the traditional authority at Linden. Whatever "desires" the workers who disagreed with the strike held in secret in their minds is of less social significance than what happened: They were not able to field a force strong enough to tilt the scales in favor of working. To put it more clearly, there were many forces at work (or not at work) in the Linden situation. The result of all these forces was the revolt. The May 1 incidents, in which tear-smoke was again used against the people, increased the authority of the revolt. The kind of remedy used is in itself a further confession that the leaders and the people live in two different worlds.

It is no purpose of this work to record the day-to-day events, except as far as they have a bearing on analysis. It should be enough to say that, in all, 21 men were arrested; 13 on charges of riot, and 8 on charges of "unlawful assembly." Outstanding among the facts of this episode is that they were all denied bail on their first appearance before the court at Wismar, a district of Linden. The event is sufficiently important to demand that the name of the Magistrate, Mr. Edward Triumph, be recorded. The Movement Against Oppression (MAO), The PPP, the Trade Union Congress (TUC) on May Day, and ASCRIA all protested against the arrests and the strong arm methods of the administration. This essay is not a record of those protests. As a result of the general new upsurge of the Linden population, the fact that all the people at Linden disagreed with the strong arm tactics, the fact that alert people everywhere thought that an affront to the working people had been committed, the fact that the TUC came out officially against the strong arm methods, all caused the police to withdraw against the strikers.

The Minister of Labor, Mr. Carrington, was becoming more and more ineffective in the situation, and lapsing more and more into those phrases that the workers had already proved to be in need of new-definition. On Sunday, May 2, 1971, he told the Press that the TUC had seen him on the Linden strike. Carrington said that "he would urge DEMBA to make payments" following the release of the report of the Tyndall Tribunal "in the shortest time possible." He said he had asked the TUC officials, who were in touch with three "leaders" of the strikers, to "impress upon them the gravity of the present situation."—what the Minister himself could not do. He asked that the strikers be told "that the situation is not in the interest of industrial democracy and stability," and that "the TUC and Consultative Association of Guyanese Industries, (CAGI) were endeavoring to maintain industrial peace for industrial stability so that all concerned could benefit." Mr. Carrington did not say what all these learned phrases really meant in the context of the Linden situation. (*Guyana Graphic*, May 3, 1971).

On May 2, the Prime Minister broadcast to the nation, addressing in particular the workers at Linden. So far as the strike itself was concerned, this broadcast was the real turning point. It promised, for the first time, that the Prime Minister would go to Linden." Subsequent to a full resumption of work at Linden," he said, "it is my intention to visit and discuss with you the issues and difficulties attendant on the nationalization of DEMBA." The May 2 broadcast is given in the documents section of this essay. It really said nothing else very new. It contained assurances like " I give you my undertaking"—but it promised that the leader and Prime Minister would visit and talk and would consult on the RILA issue.

On May 4th, newspapers reported: "END TO TWO WEEK STRIKE AT DEMBA." The *Guyana Graphic* report is given in full:

> The crippling two-weeks strike by the bauxite employees of DEMBA officially ended last night when the workers endorsed a decision by some of the leaders who emerged during the period that raised serious social and economic issues for the nation as

a whole.

Hundreds of workers, who assembled in the headquarters of the Guyana Mine Workers' Union which the striking employees have been occupying, in defiance of the union executive, for the past weeks, voted to resume work on this specific condition:

That within four weeks they will be paid the new wage rates and retroactive pay (up to February 1970), on the basis of the award to be made by the Tyndall Arbitration Tribunal.

This time limit gives the tribunal two weeks to submit the award, and DEMBA another two weeks to make the necessary pay-out.

The workers, who endorsed their leaders' decision on the advice they had received from the Guyana Trade Union Congress, dropped their demand for the immediate release of their 25 colleagues who are now in the police custody on charges for various offenses, and allow the law to take its course.

But they made it clear that they wished to have 'our comrades back with us' as within 10 minutes they had collected $1.36

Three of the 25 now in police custody are not employees of DEMBA but live and work in the Mackenzie area. Two of the three are working with a private contracting firm, while the third is a taxi driver.

The decision to endorse the back-to-work call, came as the plants of DEMBA were operating normally by the growing number of employees who kept turning up for work during the day.

The leaders of the workers, who addressed the

meeting in the absence of any official representative from the Mine Workers' Union said that 'to end the strike at this stage is a victory for us,' since, as they declared, they were able to get specific guarantees about the time-table for payment before Vesting day (the nationalization of DEMBA).

The soldiers of the GDF were no longer on patrol during yesterday, and the company said the turnout in the industrial complex was around 70 per cent.

But by four o'clock there was virtually a complete turnout with only a few workers who were out of town, being absent.

The back-to-work trek actually started around nine on Sunday night when four buses packed with workers moved away from the pullman shed towards the mines

Here the miners joined scores of other workers, who had returned to their jobs, after a series of meetings with Deputy Prime Minister Dr. P. A. Reid.

The strike leaders' decision to end the exercise followed a report, which was received from the Trades Union Council, advising that the workers be instructed to go back to work.

Last Friday the TUC was given a mandate by the workers to discuss their grievances with the Labor Minister and as a result, there followed a meeting on Sunday night between Mr. Carrington and a TUC delegation.

The strike leaders managed to get the back-to-work message to many of their supporters but the majority got the word at the Mine Workers' Union Hall before the seven o'clock siren was sounded.

Many others were satisfied with the Prime Minister's assurances and had already decided to resume work yesterday morning.
(*Guyana Graphic*, May 4, 1971.)

The Prime Minister's visit to Linden took place on May 6 and 7, 1971. These visits were very useful to the political future of Guyana, and of all black people in this hemisphere. Soon after, the Peoples National Congress began to issue pamphlets at Linden under the title "The Voice of the Real Workers," in response to the "Voice of the Workers," issued by the Committee of 10, representing the strikers. One of these pamphlets challenged the validity of the revolt:

> We all know that Government has put the facts to us and have told us the decision is ours to make as individuals. Why are others so keen to rush us into a decision by a show of hands in public? Whose interests do they really serve? We have 5,000 workers at Linden and Ituni.
>
> Can a few shouting at Cuffy Square decide for all of us? And those who want to railroad us now at public meetings and claim to have a mandate, preach about 'every man is his own leader'.
>
> Let every man decide for himself in his own home what he wants done with his pension money. Let every man wait for the Government Questionnaire and give his own answer. Nobody has a mandate to speak for us.

Another issue accused the strikers' spokesmen of being used by ALCAN which was "attempting through its agents and stooges masquerading as workers to subvert the loyalty of the Guyanese bauxite workers to the new company."

No self criticism appeared in the party handouts. Going back to the strike, another one said: "We have one strike already. Many reasons were advanced to justify it. But who did it really hurt? Did it hurt DEMBA? Did it hurt ALCAN? No it did not. It hurt the workers and it hurt Guyana." So it certainly did, but no part of the responsibility seems to be admitted.

In this same issue, the Government's theoreticians seem to have given up the original thesis that DEMBA (ALCAN) needed calcined ore so much that it could not afford to hurt or sabotage the enterprise at Linden. This point of view had been held rather strongly by certain government personalities. Now the line was changed—for a better and more realistic line.

"DEMBA is leaving reluctantly. No one gives up a good thing easily. ALCAN does not intend to give up without a fight. ALCAN is determined to destroy GUYBAUX even before it has started—if they can."

It was to be assumed, and ASCRIA had declared from the very first statement made by ALCAN, that we were at war with AL-CAN. We saw ALCAN's reply as a declaration of war again against the people. It would be strange if that imperialist octopus is not, at this very moment, dabbling at various levels in the affairs of Guyana and trying to find a footing somewhere, lobbying the US Senate, and engaging in the whole list of counter-revolutionary resorts.

By issuing pamphlets to the workers the party has made a step forward. But it failed to criticize its own shortcomings in the presence of the workers, or in writing anywhere.

Admitting faults is looked upon as losing face. But every PPP member, every white man in the city has a great deal of information on DEMBA and the roles of various actors on the stage during the April revolt.

Although there was a great deal of activity following the Prime Minister's first trip to Linden, there is no sign at all that the content of political work is richer or deeper, or more concrete.

The method of procedure, the style of work, seems to wrongly assume a politically static people who advance only at the pace set by the leaders.

Chapter Four:
The Strikers

We now come to examine the revolting group itself, and to set it in its proper social perspective. Since this question is being misrepresented or avoided, it is all the more important to discuss it with as few prejudices as possible.

The dissident workers went on strike as a means of bringing pressure to the authorities, with the object of an early payment before Vesting Day of the Tyndall Arbitration Award. When the news began to circulate that the union had not paid its barrister for presentation of the union's case before the Tyndall Tribunal, the camel's back broke. On the first days of the strike, as reported, the Minister of Labor visited the area and had discussions with various groups of workers. On their witness, their anxiety increased when the Minister of Labor Carrington, full of his lessons of the rule of law and the independence of the judiciary, told the workers that he could not "pressure the tribunal." The workers' demand to see the Prime Minister was related to this declaration by the Minister of Labor. It further confused them when, later on that Tuesday, Mr. Carrington, as previously reported, said that the monetary aspect of the award should be separated from the other aspects and promised payment of the award within two weeks. They wished to know how, without "pressuring the tribunal," the Minister could make such a promise.

It was unfortunate for the government that the April group had lost confidence in the Minister of Labor since August, 1970, during the controversy over the nurse's case. At that time, they accused the Minister of being indulgent with the union executive, who had to be pushed into a militant position.

Spokesmen of the April group very interestingly described the strike as a "social" one, with a whole bundle of objectives apart from the award. They complained about neglect by the government in the area of water supply, roads, houses. These in fact were among the demands being shouted by the strikers as they assembled below the Union Hall at Linden. They believed that the neglect they alleged was brought about by the fact that they were, considered a PNC stronghold, already in the bag, with no need to be courted.

When the strike broke out, the alumina plant was the first to close down. The strikers then massed outside the gates of the bauxite plant, in an effort at calling the workers out. By 10 a.m., they had moved to the Union Hall, for an unstated purpose. There they met Mr. Winston Verbeke, the union president who appeared to be attempting to rally support at the hall. They bombarded him with inquiries about the arbitration award, and pointedly inquired whether the union's fees had been paid. Verbeke strangely answered that he did not know, an answer which might have been bureaucratically—but not democratically—correct. This raised the fury of the workers assembled, and the union president was put under "house arrest." Either before this act or just after, the General Secretary, Mr. Benjamin, escaped by jumping through a window, and alerted the police.

At this point, they were addressed by Kwame (Martin Bobb), who asked the workers to decide on a line of action. Many of the various workers spoke freely. What the revolt had done was to cut down the " platform "—the usual pre-arranged list of speakers appointed to give guidance. Each one could speak according to his own opinion and insights. Either now or before, they had agreed on a policy: "Every man is his own leader and we are leaderless."

At any rate, this policy was re-emphasized at this meeting. It is important to attempt some comment on this slogan, which is of great significance in problems of leadership, a problem with which every association, whether political party, cooperative, or country, is faced.

The slogan, "every man is his own leader and we are lead-erless," took into account the need to let the workers know that each of them individually and collectively was responsible for the struggle. The idea of a small group representing the people, go-ing on delegations, perhaps making decisions and then reporting back to the members, did not appeal to those who would other-wise have been leaders of the revolt.

The strikers, and especially those who would have been the leaders, Maurice Frank, Desmond Moffatt (Okomfo) and Gaskin, had in practice reached a high level of political civilization. The once-for-all meeting to outline and approve strategy for the next year—or five years—places much decision-making power in the hand of the executive minority. It also causes the rank and file to go to sleep, leaving their whole destiny in the hands of the "lead-ers." When a crisis comes, they confront the leaders with a whole volume of just and unjust questions. Since there were no "lead-ers," meetings had to be held frequently, at each turn of events or each possibility of a turn. Scores of workers therefore had to meet frequently to decide on tactics for the next day or next half day. Another reason for this was that the group assumed that there were people among them who were giving information to the police. The only way to avoid being betrayed beforehand to the police was to take decisions not long ahead of the time for acting on the decisions.

At the meeting in the Union Hall on April 19, following the release of Verbeke by the police, it was decided that the strikers should walk to the city the next day to see the Prime Minister. That, it appears, is how the meeting came to decide also on an invitation to the Prime Minister to be present by midnight with the ultimatum "or else," a phrase coined by Burnham in 1961. The idea was to fix the supposed time of the Prime Minister's visit to fit in with the proposal for a walk to the city. The word came back that the Prime Minister had hung up the phone on the workers sent to convey the workers' message. The messenger (Okomfo) from his political orientation or philosophy—he is perhaps the first example of a worker revolutionary, from the strict class point of view—would not have regarded the message to the Prime Minister as anything other than the highest law, as it was a decision of workers over which he would have no power. He would also sincerely regard it as binding on the Prime Minister as well.

Because of the report that the Prime Minister, after a short conversation, and after saying "I heard you" twice to the caller from Linden, had put down the phone caused the workers to decide to call off the idea of a visit to Georgetown, and make the visit of the Prime Minister to Linden the main issue. Just before Mr. Carrington arrived on the scene from Georgetown, the workers had come together and resolved not to return to work as a result of appeals the Minister, or anyone else, might make. The spokesman of the revolt made the point that a new fact of the April strike was the full solidarity of the alumina plant. Such was the determination of the strikers that some 300 workers were then massed outside the bauxite plant gate.

The kind of communication that took place between Mr. Carrington and the workers is already dealt with in Chapter 3, which records the government's conduct of its business during the April Revolt. We can go back to follow the revolt itself. By Tuesday evening the revolt was beginning to feel its strength. The workers again gathered at the Union Hall, but did nothing new except, it appears, to decide to continue the strike and to attempt to widen the strike the next day. But so certain were they that the Prime Minister would come in and answer their ultimatum, that some 25 remained in the Union Hall all night, just in case he arrived at a late hour. In this context, it was decided to implement a previous opinion that if Burnham did not turn up, the leader of the opposition, Cheddi Jagan, should be invited. The main reason for this decision was, in a desperate situation, to bring political pressure of a very necessary kind to the government. The argument was that Jagan was invited not as a party, but as a parliamentary opposition leader—next to the Prime Minister, the most powerful man in Parliament. Since the Nationalization Bill had been passed by Parliament, and vesting day was to be fixed by the government, and since consultations between the government and opposition were going on, they considered it an important form of pressure to open the door of Linden to Jagan. It is quite clear though, that PPP members at Linden, a very tiny minority, welcomed the invitation to Jagan for other political reasons. To them, including those, if any, in the strike leadership, it was a real triumph. Later on, expelled members of the committee of the revolt accused others of PPP leanings.

The invitation to the PPP leader, in the words of Ndugu Kwame Apata, was not a political swing to the PPP, but a sign that workers were now prepared to manipulate politicians as politicians had always manipulated workers in the past. There is no sign at all that workers at Linden have swung towards the PPP But during the revolt it was clear that a type of PPP line of attack on the government had become bolder in that area than it had ever been. In the climate of Linden, the PPP activists would have tried to hide this attachment, except in the case of a breakdown of mass confidence in the PNC.

The Prime Minister did not arrive. Next morning, Wednesday, there were some 1000 workers on the streets trying to prevent a turn out by other non-striking sections. All the time, the question of the Prime Minister's coming was with the people and as time passed became a more and more important demand.

During Wednesday and Thursday, the spokesmen of the revolt took strong exception to a release by the Wismar Compound of ASCRIA that accused the strikers of inviting the man (Jagan), who had been Prime Minister at the time of the Son Chapman launch disaster which had left pregnant women floating in the

Demerara River. The revolt spokesmen protested that "race was being used." The revolt very purely expressed alarm that the Son Chapman incident, in which PPP members caused the death of some 30 innocent Africans by setting a time bomb to the Son Chapman launch as it left Georgetown for Mackenzie, with a complement of bauxite workers and their families, should be recalled at this time.

On Wednesday night, April 20, the owner of the Son Chapman launch, Mr. Chapman, a Linden businessman, was asked by the revolt to intervene with the Prime Minister and try to get him to come to Linden. The Prime Minister, who was most anxious to please, it would seem, complained of a crowded schedule and invited a delegation to meet him at his home in Belfield, about 16 miles east of Georgetown. The invitation was refused. The rumor said that it was because of fear of arrest that the partisans of the revolt refused to elect a delegation for Belfield. The main spokesman of the revolt, however had other objectives: "Every man is a leader and we are leaderless." Under that philosophy, they were willing to go to Belfield only if all the workers could go along. On these grounds the Belfield project fell through.

The revolt itself was using short term methods of organization. Already, the mass democracy is no longer a form of organization with them. At the time of the revolt too, the tempers of the workers were so high that no one wanted to be accountable to them for things done in their absence.

On Friday of the first week of the strike, the bauxite kilns began smoking. About 200 employees were back on the job. The task was actually being accomplished under the initiative of the ASCRIA compound, who saw the shut down of the bauxite works, now that the nationalization bill had been passed, as a crime against the nation. It was also the first time that they had acted publicly against the spokesmen of the revolt, with whom they had always a large area of agreement. Being black revolutionaries in particular, as opposed to worker-revolutionaries in general, the ASCRIA Compound placed the emphasis on support for and confidence in a government carrying out a revolutionary act. The April revolt was concerned with the position of the workers in that situation and was, in fact, by means of its pressure, giving new instructions of great value to the government, and to all who were capable of learning. The ASCRIA - Wismar Compound, along with such elements of the PNC as could function at all, waged a heroic struggle to keep the enterprise from closing down.

Saturday brought a continuation of Friday's trends, but moreover, a rumor that the Prime Minister would make a statement. There was widespread interest in the statement, and a meeting of the workers was fixed for Wednesday at 9 a.m. The workers, after discussing the published statement, rejected it. They objected to the argument that it was "immaterial" whether the money was paid out before vesting day. The use of such a word at that distance, between Belfield and Linden, some hundred miles by road witnessed more than anything else the great communication gulf that existed between the leaders and their people. It is named in this essay, on page 1, as one of the institutions overthrown[1] by the April revolt.

The workers believed that "immaterial" was used to throw them off the scent, to get them to drop their guard, and not to care whether or not the money was paid before vesting day, and not to insist on payment of the award being made before vesting day. It is more likely that the Prime Minister intended by the use of the word "immaterial" that the workers need not worry, need not be concerned whether vesting day came first of the payment of the award came first, as the workers would receive the award as a

---

1   When it is said that an institution (party system, trade union system, etc.) was "overthrown," it is not meant that the institution is no longer in use. The statement means that an event has shown clearly that the institution or method is no longer valid, up-to-date, or suited to the task.

direct payment to them in either case. The spokesmen also made the point that they were somewhat afraid of Mr. Burnham's power with language.

As remarked before, a most interesting feature of the spokesmen of the revolt was their resistance to the temptation to become leaders. The workers were very anxious for them to put on this mantle. In developing countries there is a great temptation to people, not only young people, to become leaders of organizations. This is one of the ready avenues of upward mobility in these societies. The successful party official, if he cares, and the successful trade union official, if he cares, can break all the social barriers that would otherwise confront him, and rise to the highest circles of society where he is used as a guinea pig, a sounding board and a source of information for spies. Chosen women are put around him to charm him, work on him, even love him—this refers mainly to European women—and keep him well-documented and indoctrinated. The officials find ways of funding themselves so that they are always able to afford anything. They may get themselves cars, not average cars, but cars fitting their new found status; and vote themselves high salaries to allow them to "live." This big living is another rope for their neck, as it very effectively cuts them off from their roots and causes them to engage in rounds of useless priorities. Hence, if a man has come to the country to do a course of lectures at the University of Guyana on "The Anteater of the Guyana Jungle"—a topic he does not necessarily know anything about—before he gives the lecture, his embassy throws a cocktail party at which they can impress their presence even more effectively on people. Our newly arrived socialites are bound to be there, picking up all the latest tips in up-to-date living. The foreign guest, when introduced to them say "O, Mr. _____ I have been told that I must see you..." We have to be thankful that there are still some trade unionists who turn their backs on these temptations.

The behavior of previous executives in the union had quite sickened the activists of the revolt. They did not, in their mind, wish to thrust leadership on the people. They wanted the leadership phase to run so that leaders could develop from among the people. But, they would expect that a new phase could be reached at which functionaries must be identified to fill the bureaucratic positions which might be vacant in the course of time. Then the problem of the cult of the leader would again face them.

As a link between the phase when "every man is a leader and we are leaderless," and the next phase, when they must take charge of the union, the workers elected a Committee of Ten. They all had to be union members, because the workers, in taking over the hall, appeared to be claiming to be the moral authority in the union, with moral power. Bobb, having been expelled from the union during the Nurse's strike, could not be a member of the 10 man committee. This committee was constituted on May 4, the day of the release from prison of the arrested workers. It continued to act only on the basis of collective decision. No man decided for the committee. There were a secretary and a treasurer, but each meeting elected a chairman for the meeting. At no time had an overwhelming majority of the strikers shown any disloyalty to the government. What they did, in effect, was to accuse the government of letting them down, as they understood it, in the early stage of the strike. They more than once declared support for Burnham, while remaining critical of some areas of government behavior, and of the man himself. This is a very vibrant democracy and should be assessed in this way. But anti-nationalization voices, since they could not operate either with the PNC or within ASCRIA, found a place within the ranks of the strikers and tried to win their point mainly by noisy shouting of anti-nationalization, and anti-ETB remarks. As explained before, the imperialist firm, which after all adopted methods suited to the particular case, waged its war on that level by "educating" the mass of the workers to feel that their delayed benefits were somehow part of the assets of the company, and if they were not paid before vesting day, they would be confiscated by the government. The government was in search of cruder forms of provocation, like bribery of the strike leaders. Do not let us forget that imperialists, having provided the background for lack of confidence, were quite content to allow the strikers with a genuine grievance to achieve one of the partial objectives without meddling. The correct analysis for the imperial role seems to be that they stood ready to meddle if necessary, as they did on the mines when they thought that efforts to keep them open were likely to succeed.

The aim of the workers was to win their awards before vesting day. In their activity, they were dealing with a particular social situation. They did not know that their activity was a signal shot for the more advanced stages of the economic revolution throughout the country. The old trade union and party system, together with the system of communications that sustained them, had all snapped at Linden, where the old institutions were under the greatest amount of pressure. The activity of the April revolt, in filling a vacuum, served the remarkable purpose of trying to teach us what the future institutions ought to be like.

We cannot afford to lose sight of the most important fact that the April revolt took place within the setting of imperialist propaganda. Since February 1970, the wage negotiations between the Guyana Mineworkers Union and DEMBA had been going on. In the earlier stage of the negotiations in 1970, when the company refused to accept the workers' demands, the issue was sent to conciliation. This means that the Ministry of Labor took a direct hand in attempting to settle the dispute. Once a Guyana government is in the saddle, it cannot encourage an economic strike, even against an imperialist firm. First, in the case of DEMBA, each day off means a loss of revenues. Next, the government is confident that it has the means of solving any dispute, and in the last analysis, the power to enforce decisions on the company. The Prime Minister's theory is that energetic agitation and strikes, in a situation in which the government is able and willing to throw its might behind the workers, should be out of place, since it weakens the very government financially. The PNC government record of coming out on the side of workers was better than the PPP's. The sugar workers, mainly (East) Indian, can testify to the many times when government imposed solutions in their favor. So too in bauxite, but without the knowledge of the rank and file.

But Burnham preferred not to let his right hand know what his left hand did. This quality is admirable on a personal level, but a Prime Minister so much in need of a good report can, by default, help the imperialist to ruin the confidence of the workers in his leadership and position. The imperialist companies continually advertise their "good works." If Burnham had taken the credit due to him in bauxite wage negotiations, the GMWU would have long been exposed in the eyes of the workers. By these and other means, the union executive was held up by false props against the will of the workers. This approach to politics in the age of confrontation with imperialism is hopelessly simple and ought to be discarded without delay. This is not saying that the Prime Minister is by any means a model revolutionary. It is simply saying that his positive side up to the time of the revolt was not sufficiently known. Political leaders must be given full credit for their positive contributions. Then their supporters will see the exact area of weakness.

To return to the history of the wage dispute from conciliation, where agreement was not reached, the dispute was sent to arbitration in October. Under the law, the arbitration procedure is very valuable. It can only be applied with the consent of both parties to the dispute. In the present case, DEMBA refused to go to arbitration because the decision of the tribunal would be binding on both the union and the company. In order to speed up a solution, the Prime Minister threatened to send the wages dispute to arbitration by special legislation. At this point, DEMBA gave in and reluctantly agreed to arbitration. It is well known that the arbitration took five months, and that the workers' confidence broke under the strain of waiting.

ALCAN's active propaganda against nationalization, or any form of participation, began in November of 1970, when the Prime Minister announced that the negotiations with ALCAN would begin on December 7, 1970, and that there were certain issues not open to negotiation. These issues were:

> (1) That government's participation shall be a majority one;
>
> (2) That participation would be by means of purchase of a share of the assets of the company;
>
> (3) That the value of such assets shall be no greater than that given by the company as the written down book value for income tax purposes on the 31st December, 1969, with additions of value during 1970, not by re-valuations or reappraisals;
>
> (4) That the government will pay for its share of the assets out of future profits of the joint undertaking, after tax;
>
> (5) That the government's majority holding shall confer on the government the control which inheres in such majority holding;
>
> (6) That the agreement finally arrived at, between the company and government, shall be deemed to take effect from 1st January, 1971.

ALCAN's reaction to this was calculated in part to give the

workers at Linden a sense of insecurity. This was the line ALCAN took all the time in relation to the workers in trying to influence the course of events. The company's response to the government's invitation to negotiate on participation was a threatened boycott of the organized new enterprise in which the government had a majority holding. ALCAN said it was attending the talks for the purposes of clarification. It declared that it would guarantee the employment of its workers, in case supplies were not available from Mackenzie.

DEMBA then began to "educate" the workers. It told them that if the government controlled the company by a majority share, the wages of the workers would be reduced; that there would be an end to their comparatively high wage rates and that their wages would be pegged, as in the case of government employees.

When on February 23, 1971, the Prime Minister announced the nationalization of DEMBA, every observer sensed the deep approval of all Guyana. At steel band tramps and drumming sessions the same day the announcement was celebrated in song.[2]

The workers at DEMBA, no less than other Guyanese, accepted nationalization politically. The DEMBA workers, since 1965, after the PNC victory, had been talking of the nationalization of DEMBA and were always posing questions of exactly how DEMBA would be decolonized. Nationalization, therefore, was not a step too revolutionary or too far reaching for their acceptance. They fully accepted nationalization politically.

But they could not really accept it industrially, because they were not helped to see, from stage to stage, how they fitted into the new arrangements. This was a question that called for political

---

2   One of these was a parody of an old emancipation song and ran: "Nationalization bill go pass, Bakra man sa eat long grass." Another: "DEMBA loss, DEMBA loss, DEMBA loss e bauxite, Fine am Burnham, fine am, fine am leh we see."

leadership and vision, which the PNC machinery at DEMBA, and at the center, did not provide and probably could not provide. It is no use drawing the conclusion, as the PNC leadership did, that it was the machinery at Linden only that failed. After all, in terms of PNC structure the activity at Linden is centrally regulated. It is impossible that a serious party will leave the fortunes of its most advanced stronghold to an MP whose strong points and limitations have always been well known. The collapse at Linden was merely a reflection of the overall condition of the party. It snapped where the pressure was greatest. That is all.

During the hot fortnight, the party groups at Linden were outpaced by the spontaneous organization of the people themselves, at first of a number of workers. Again, the party retained the political loyalty of the overwhelming majority of the workers, and the rest of the people, especially before the repressions, but it did not retain their operational loyalty. They resented its interference in the industrial management. The dynamic forces were moving in other directions and took the people along with them.

An accurate examination of positions of the various groups at work in the situation is very necessary for clarification and for the future development of the people's movement in Guyana. There will be objections that such a thing should not be set out in black and white. This objection can be easily answered: The whites who controlled DEMBA at the time of the strike knew almost every aspect of the situation, because they were on the spot and because they had worked and hoped for something worse, and were therefore fully aware of every aspect of the situation through their spies and agents. The PPP, following, was fairly well informed on the day to day incidents of the strike through the *Mirror*, Jagan's daily newspaper. It suited the *Mirror* to do this because it was a way of attacking the government and of trying to make capital of the government's blunders. The only people who were badly informed about the day to day incidents were the PNC members and followers, who had to rely on the daily morning newspapers for incomplete reports.

The members were confused. They had on the spot no real front line political people, in the creative sense. The leadership there was comprised of people, outstanding for their loyalty and accomplishments as election canvassers and fund raisers, but had never been asked to be responsible for much else—most of whose practical sharpness arose from their confrontation with imperialism, rather than from direct political education.

The strike was called against a background of discontent with the government's view that the accumulated funds of the company pension scheme (RILA) should not be distributed to the workers, but held for the sake of continuity and for the workers' benefits in a central fund after the repatriation of the money from Canada. The government felt that nothing should be done to relieve ALCAN of paying over its accumulated RILA contribution to the Guyanese organization. But it was not the RILA proposal that was the main issue of the strike and of the return-to-work negotiations. It was the question of the delay of payment of wage increases due since early 1970, and, which is much the same thing, the delay of the Tyndall tribunal in announcing its award on wages and other conditions of work. At a stormy union meeting in the new Union Hall at Linden on April 15, the union leaders are reported to have taken an anti-government line, tending to suggest that the government was to blame for the delay. A PNC supporter, prominent in the area, then revealed to the meeting that the union's final argument to the tribunal had not been presented by the union's lawyers, since the union had not yet paid the lawyers fees. This news infuriated the workers, who were already critical of the use of the union dues—which amounted to some $2,500 a week—by the union leadership. The PNC member who revealed the information of the non-payment of lawyer's fees has been criticized by his comrades for causing the strike. His retort is that he revealed the information in order to save the government undeserved attack.

The PNC saw the strike as an expression of disloyalty by the workers. These leaders had been, up to the day before the strike, away from the scene at the PNC's 14th Annual Congress, which lasted for a week and which had been a serious attempt to deal with all issues of government policy. The Congress was organized on a very enlightened basis. PNC Ministers, as usual, put forward papers on issues of government economic policy. There was much, though not enough time, for discussions in workshops, and very excellent members' participation in these workshops, as seen by the reports of the workshops to the full sessions. In addition to this, two district leaders of the party, who were asked to present papers, were moderately critical of the functioning of the party's "middle management," but they did not touch the hierarchy, that is the most highly placed leaders. One group's report was very critical of the attitude of a high party official. It attacked him with the charge of ostentatious living, a charge that a few party officials will have to face up to before long. The party official concerned said that he " did not understand" the criticisms. A workshop criticism of the government's policy on interior development, including the closing down of interior co-ops by cutting off of financial support, drew no reply from the leadership. In addition to this program of papers, discussions, and workshops, there was a program of community work in which all delegates participated, including those from the Caribbean, Zambia, Barbados, and Tanzania. Organizationally, looking at the conference itself, there could be few better organized meetings anywhere. The level of participation was also good. Insofar as the scope of discussion and examination of government policy went, the party set a new tradition for Guyana, the rest of the Caribbean, and for many parts of Africa and Asia. But there was no real calling to account of Ministers. Any such thing drew a quick defense from the platform.

To district leaders returning to Linden from such an experience, a strike of the bauxite workers must have seemed treachery. The isolation between the two events, the fact that both, though important, were unconnected organizationally, leads to interesting conclusions: that the party organization at Linden does not include a most vibrant body of the bauxite workers; that a most vibrant body of workers at Linden do not feel at one with the district PNC leadership; that the PNC at Linden is lacking in revolutionary mood and does not provide the right climate for a most vibrant group of the working people.

During the days of the revolt the established organizations were under siege. ASCRIA had decided, from the blackbaiting of 1970, not to take the initiative in labor disputes or in the political thrust, since such action had caused it to be labeled subversive by conservative supporters, by the PPP, and by the white population. At all times, the more enlightened people in the PNC, and in the country, had understood ASCRIA's organs. ASCRIA, at Linden, was therefore, at the time, in a state of self-imposed paralysis on the industrial front, and limited itself to a certain role. The trade union had, in effect, collapsed. The union executives could not hold the union office, nor could they show their faces on the street, nor address the workers on strike, nor talk to regional party leaders, whom they blamed for causing the strike. It was the workers in revolt who held sway during those fifteen days.

We should also recognize one fact. When political events like this take place involving a crisis, and there is an apparent solution, the period after the crisis is never the same again. The new authority gained by the workers during the crisis, developed as a result of trends and causes that existed long before. And the new authority, thus historically developed and becoming publicly known during the crisis, will continue to play a role in the new period, so that the power relations are never the same again. Any attempt at repression of the new authority will result in equally long term instability of the social unit. Insofar as the April revolt was revolutionary, it is the task of the political movement to learn from it and to use the experience to develop its overall and particular revolutionary ideology and policy. This is how political theory in a given country must be enriched and made realistic by the noting and studying of general lessons from experience.

The role of the ASCRIA compound in Wismar (Linden) in the April revolt is one that needs to be carefully explained. For one thing, no serious person has now claimed that "ASCRIA is at the bottom of it." People, but not serious people, have claimed this. Some very clever persons saw in the whole thing the burning desire of the Coordinating Elder to make himself Prime Minister. If without a party, without an army and without force of any kind, and with membership of an organization drawn only from among the African people, the Coordinating Elder of ASCRIA seriously seeks to make himself Prime Minister, then it is time to cease all other analysis and have his head examined by a team of experienced psycho-analysts and specialists in all kinds of lunacy. The conduct of the ASCRIANs in Linden in April sprang from the basic experience and the decisions of 1970 and the nurse's strike.

It had been agreed with the Wismar Compound at that time, that all appearance of meddling in union affairs, all attempts at competing with the official union executive, would be interpreted as unfriendly to the party, and as an attempt to wrest leadership from it and from the union. The Coordinating Elder had argued quite clearly then that the Verbeke clique could not possibly survive but that "a crisis could mature" seeing that the unpopular leaders had not undergone any change of outlook. The bankruptcy of the Union Executive is seen from the fact that it had to yield control of the union office, control of the most vibrant part of the labor force and control of the streets to members whom it had expelled just eight months before.

The view of the April revolt taken by members of the ASCRIA Compound was that the strike was a mistake, in view of the fact that the Nationalization Act had been passed by Parliament. It did not share the profound loss of confidence in the government expressed by many of the workers on strike. As Black revolutionaries, the members have been trained to have confidence in Black leaders, thus overcoming generations of lack of faith which has bedeviled our communities for centuries. They know that African people in Guyana, unlike all other race groups, are willing to be influenced by any rumor about their leaders, whether the rumor is absurd or not. Part of our activity, therefore, is to strengthen Black people against this kind of sickness, much exploited by supposed revolutionaries of other races, making deliberate use of this weakness of our people. However, since the black revolutionaries have as much analytical skill and ideological knowledge as anyone else, we are not going to accept the line of known opportunists, racists, and frustrated intellectuals on this score. The ASCRIA Compound at Wismar, therefore, had assumed the sincerity of the Prime Minister and leader of the PNC, quite ignoring other ministers. In this point, it was much clearer than in the ambivalence shown by the strikers, who were mercilessly critical of the Burnham government but vocally full of faith in the Prime Minister.

Some people have argued, in the course of discussion, somewhat like this: If the strike resulted in part from imperialist propaganda, how then can it be claimed that the institutions were at fault? The answer is that the imperialist propaganda took fully into account the type of institutions and their fighting condition. From this we can draw another lesson: the imperialist spies nowadays study very carefully the people and their responses. This is now priority material for agents. Hospitality to foreign whites, who seem to drop from the skies, should therefore be out of the question. All these Oxford scholars and Wayne assistant professors who want to study village life should be given no assistance by the people. It is obvious, too, that where whites find they are unwelcome, they will select blacks for use as agents. What happened at Linden was that the imperialists, in choosing their line of propaganda, took note of the poor state of the institutions and directed the propaganda to suit. Perhaps they also correctly expected an anti-popular response from the political leaders.

The members of the leadership of the revolt were serious thinkers. They began by voting that new methods were necessary to deal with the situation. They tried out new forms of organization. The fact that the workers' committee filled a gap in the process of life does not say that it was the form that will best serve the new situation. What is important is that it showed the capacity of alienated workers for self assertion, self-determination, for responding to situations, and for creative development of workers' government. Such workers are, in quality, ready for socialism and ready to defend it.

Chapter Five:
Outsiders

One of the institutions challenged—and in reality over-thrown—by the April revolt was the communications system. In many ways it can be argued that the nature of the communications system was one of the factors bringing about the April revolt. That communications system, in its turn, was developed historically. It resulted from our experiences, from our education and lack of it; and it is rooted socially in the colonial class system, which is also a racial system. In order to explain this claim, it will be necessary to trace our historical communications experience, and see by what means ideas and information have been communicated to the people. This brief inquiry should also help us to decide what the relationship between authority and the people has been at each stage.

In times of slavery, the ruling class of white slave owners, or their representatives on the spot, took decisions about production and the regulation of life. We can explore the means by which the people became aware of these decisions. It would be obvious that the "top management" itself seldom had any direct contact with the slaves in a body. The slaves were divided into gangs. Each gang was under the control of a driver, and a few groups would come under the control of the overseer. For effective communication, the supervisory staff—the middle management—was best recruited from the ranks of the blacks. The slaves who formed the driver class were doubtless those who better understood the language of the rulers, but had not lost touch with the people. This principle, by the way, seemed to hold and will hold while any kind of alienation remains a feature of the society. It is a system by which an alienated society can be efficiently run for a time.

This method of contact between the top management of

slavery and the enslaved population was further refined by the introduction of the men of God, who by and large provided an effective means of communication with, and indoctrination of, the slaves. In view of the slave revolution of 1763, and the numerous other uprisings, it was not surprising that the church, using what would then be grassroots methods, preached a doctrine of peace, and of love for the enemy. In our history, this seems to be the earliest example of secondary communication. This phrase is intended to describe a situation in which the main communicator has developed a self-acting agency for giving information, and for teaching and understanding of the rules. This agency, although self acting, understood (perhaps better than the ruling group itself) the general propaganda needs of the ruling group. The tendency was therefore, that in work situations, communication was left to the middle management; but then the communication of ideas and the stimulation of attitudes were left largely to the missionaries, with their more total grasp of the situation. The churchmen relied not only on the Church, but on the schools, which later on developed a fairly efficient system of mind control. It is interesting that the colonial period has come and gone, the age of independence has come, but no serious effort has been made to liberate our minds. No serious attempt has been made to give us a new non-colonial image of the Amerindians, of the Africans, nor of the Indians from the East. The political elite fail, in the first place, to liberate their own mind. To some extent, all of us are victims of our own failure to liberate our minds.

Leaving slavery aside, we come to the colonial period proper. Here we come to a period in which the state becomes strengthened relative to the plantations. The state takes on the overall management of the country in the interest of the capitalist class. There is a whole series of institutions developed for the purposes of teaching the official doctrine and of exercising various controls. The state also permits private enterprise in the field of propaganda and communication: high schools, missions, learned societies, the press and later on the radio—all of these developed more or less independently and under the inspiration of private enterprise and the British Empire. From time to time, many specific interests found it necessary to establish their own means of communication with the people for definite objectives. Some of these were complementary to the existing system, and some at various times were considered subversive of it. Groups that rose up and found their interest at war with the colonial objectives, or at war with the state and official culture, set up their own means of communication for their own objectives: newspapers, the East Indian Association, various Indian religious organizations, the African Society, The Popular Party, the Negro Progress Convention, farmers associations, church guilds and movements, and perhaps the most earth shaking of them all in those days, the trade union.

The struggles of the waterfront workers, in which Critchlow played an outstanding part, were certainly a significant breakthrough in communications. Their influence spread to rural areas. As recently as the 1950s there were rural workers alive who remembered having joined Critchlow's union. These struggles developed a working man's ideology on which the 1953 political movement was able to build. What is most interesting, however, is the means of communication between "leaders" and followers. Critchlow's methods seemed to have been methods of mass politics.

This activity of Critchlow and his comrades left a deep impression on the working masses. On important occasions, he used to organize marches in which workers tramped the streets singing the Internationale. Such times have not been since those days. The effect of Critchlow's trade union activity was to imbue the workers with a consciousness of their conditions which smashed the absurd illusion of prosperity and well being fostered by the colonial institutions. But the main thing: the people had taken part in forming a most important organization and in establishing a new communications culture.

It was the age of mass political activity that developed the types of communications, from about 1947, which are relevant to the DEMBA events. These forms began to be important on a haphazard basis in the 1950s. One remembers Cheddi Jagan, during a local government election campaign in the city, charging into "the sugar producers and the Wight family." One remembers Burnham, soon after his return from England, speaking to a huge mass meeting at Bourda Green and explaining how the world had changed—"look at China…"—and achieving an electric effect. CLR James some time later talked about the mass political meetings in the developing countries and compared them with the general lack of interest in meetings in the advanced countries. The Caribbean was perhaps the outstanding land of the public meeting where at Bourda Green, at the University of Woodford Square, and in other familiar meeting places, a very high percentage of our small population gathered to prepare for the new times that were demanded.

Public education spread rapidly through the agency of the mass public meeting. By the middle fifties, people learned who the enemy was, they knew what was in the way of change, and they could reach agreement on how to attack the problem of change. It was through this agency that the latent individual protest against imperialism became grouped into a social force and formalized into a line of struggle and way of life. Where the overwhelming majority of the people are below the poverty line, and where the new political leaders had to deal with the residue of the working man's ideology of Critchlow's times, and with the previous anti-crown colony positions of Dargan, Weber, Crane, as well as with the recent martyrdom of the Enmore workers (1948), it was possible for many political parties to be established. Those supported by the masses were those that presented a working class concern and an anti-colonialist program.

Together with the mass public meetings, in the old days, there were many week-end training schools in which large numbers of party leaders in the PPP (led by Jagan and Burnham) were trained in a political ideology in which Martin Carter, Sydney King (now Eusi Kwayana), and Ramkarran took a leading part, along with Jagan and Burnham. After the split, there began to be an increasing difference between the principles laid down in the early days and the practice of the leader, Dr. Jagan, who took a direct racialist path on major issues, such as West Indian Federation.

We have looked, then, at the means by which at first authority and then the people's movement itself, communicated with the people. There had been famous people's movements as far back as in the 18th century—for example, the 1763 revolution and afterward. They had been faced with major difficulties of communication because of the absolute nature of the government of the day. But the fact of their segregation was perhaps a factor that outweighed the police system, whatever it was.

The type of communications system that helped the PNC win is the same type that became established in the late 1940s, and reached all important propositions in the 1960s, and in some aspect has prevailed into the 1970s. It prevailed *in some way* because there have in fact been important modifications. The political parties generally kept up the pressure of public mass meetings until the time of general elections. Tons of political literature helped the public meetings. After elections, the whole pace died down. This is perhaps evidence that the parties are not so much parties of government as election parties. As is to be expected between two election parties, it is the opposition party that is more than active in the area of public meetings. All of a sudden, the 100,000 people or so who could, in the course of a week spend about between 3 and 5 hours at such meetings, "learning to govern," at the feet, so to speak, of the leading political minds of the country, were suddenly cut off from all political education. The victorious politicians, busy with ministerial and parliamentary work, cannot, or do not, spare much time for the activities that were so necessary to bring them to office. Instead of communicating with the public through the public meeting as before, the leaders have relied on the news media, the press and the radio. Most of them have accepted the opinion that the media, with its press reports, press releases, and photographs, and its broadcasts and interviews, are a good enough replacement for the public meeting. It may even be argued that they are more efficient than the public meeting, since in five minutes of radio time it is possible to touch all Guyanese, where as in five minutes of a public meeting only at best a few tens of thousands can be affected. Yet there are obvious objections to the media, as opposed to the more personal relationship of the public meeting. There, at the meeting, the agitator or propagandist speaking to the crowd was able to get the people's response on the spot, to sense their questions, doubts, fears, to learn from them, and to benefit from a unique experience. The media leaves things cold. No one can talk back to a newspaper or seriously heckle a radio broadcast.

The public mass meeting, as a form of democratic participation, may not last for all time. When such agencies as television, and even radio, are within the grasp of every other household, interest in public mass meetings is very likely to fall for a number of reasons. The politician, too, considers it less exerting and more economic to appear on the media than to be in many places at one time. Through media, he gets a sort of omnipresence, which can help to dull his senses. The politician is seen by masses of people without his seeing their faces or hearing their comments. The public meeting has indeed severe limitations. But it is unequaled as a direction giver, as a mood tester, as a solidarity builder, as a means of communication between so called leaders and followers, or supporters. Still, it is no substitute either for the party cell or the classroom.

In almost giving up the public meeting as a vehicle of communication with the public, the PNC leadership no doubt expected more activity to take place in districts and in the cells. The people have not been given an ideology based on an interpretation of history. The groups, and this goes for the PPP as well, do not consider themselves organs of any kind of revolution, but merely agencies for securing or maintaining the political power represented by their leader being the Prime Minister. Because of these serious limitations, the groups do not mobilize their districts, as they have nothing around which to mobilize them.

Now look again at the demand of the workers to see their leader in person.

The explosion at Linden came about in the following circumstances. The old method of political communication had been discarded and nothing had been put in its place. Political activity of the popular political groups can both explain alienation and reduce its effects. When political activity fails to do this, we must face the consequences of that alienation, which has no reason for hope.

Chapter Six:
After Gaff

The Wismar compound of ASCRIA, during the April days, played a patriotic role. It saw nationalization as an international war and did not think it wise to strike between the passage of the Nationalization Bill (which empowered the Government to take over firms in the bauxite industry), and Vesting Day, the day of taking possession. It could afford to take that position because of its faith in black people and in an African Prime Minister who had given his word. The ASCRIA members came out on strike for the sake of workers' solidarity, but after Carrington's proposals, they called for an end to the strike.

The Council of Elders did not agree that the strike was desirable, but had to regard it as something that could not be avoided. Whereas the Wismar compound was involved in the internal conflict among the workers, the Council of Elders could take a less partisan or less factional view. The problem of the Wismar compound was what to do when they thought it was time for the strike to end.

The Wismar Compound spent ceaseless energies helping to organize work and continue production so as to reverse the strike. It succeeded only in part. It also had the responsibility of not moving away from the PNC groups in the area, with which it had been already having problems of competition. Being not limited by the political restraints of government and the PNC on questions of African development, African culture, social revolution and the need to multi-racialize the party, ASCRIA *ndugu*[1] had everywhere a clear and more definite unapologetic ideology and position. If the Wismar compound of ASCRIA had joined the April revolt, the

---

1   Kiswahili word that translates to "comrades" - ed.

action would have led to a major split. Statements made by the Council of Elders were on a different level. We declared that the workers had grievances and called for the intervention of government to end the strike by hastening the arbitration award. After the arrest and tear-smoking, ASCRIA attacked the Prime Minister's political and civil service advisers for leading him up the garden path, and for advising neocolonialist methods of dealing with workers' problems.

The argument of this writing is that the strike was the solution by those who had lost confidence in the trade union system, the political system, and the system of communications. The strikers continued to proclaim their confidence in the Prime Minister, whom they called "the leader of the workers;" but the Prime Minister is only a person, not a system. It is also our argument that the trade union system, the political system, and system of communications had been left behind by events.

Nowhere in the independent countries of the Caribbean have authentic working class men risen to the ranks of national leadership. Even if one or two do—as has happened in Antigua—without a workers' ideology, his rise would be entirely useless. The innocently bourgeois structure of all the political parties, both government and opposition, the PPP in Guyana included, has made it impossible for working class cadres to emerge as national leaders. We are talking in the context of the customary political party that regards the people as an audience, as secondary, and the "leader" as primary. The professional class, a significant social stratum in the Caribbean, has often played the role of a national bourgeoisie. So far, the leaders seem to spring from among the lower middle classes. In a few cases—Jamaica for example—sometimes from wealthy West Indian groups, and they are chiefly responsible for the preservation of whatever colonial institutions remain at the economic, cultural or ideological levels. Without knowing it, and chiefly because they are afraid of the people and spend so little time educating the people in the spirit of true independence, they are actively preserving, without examination or correction, those institutions which do most violence to the idea of total liberation.

Mere poverty or mere working class origin of the leadership is not a safe guide to whether a party is under revolutionary guidance. Some of these leaders have had no education but the official colonial and neocolonial education. In these cases, their leadership of the people makes imperialist rule easier for some time. The environment, the society, and the social climate are important agencies in the creation of committed activists and revolutionaries.

The opposition party in Guyana, the Peoples' Progressive Party, has gained fame as a revolutionary party by its flaunting of the ready-made formulations of Marxism-Leninism, or to be more exact, of the Soviet Communist Party. Because the PPP deliberately proposes the Soviet Foreign Policy, the world—thanks to the mass media—has somehow got the impression that the PPP is the least conventional of all parties, based on scientific analysis and a revolutionary break with the past. This assumption is quite false. The PPP leaders live by the law of bourgeois aspiration. They are caught up in the traditional lifestyle of the new elite. The party is, in terms of the needs of the people, in terms of the revolutionary temper of the bulk of population, a reactionary party. It no more organizes the people to rule themselves than do the other parties of the region.

The revolutionary party of today must not organize people merely for elections and for fund-raising. The party must equip the people with an ideology of change. In the course of teaching this ideology, the people will make important contributions to the development of the ideology and program. It is the collective experience of the oppressed people at home and abroad that is the best raw material for an ideology. Planning and decision making over wide areas should then become the main function of the basic regional party organs. Parties in the first world which fail to practice true revolutionary democracy are running into trouble with their people. The material and mental condition of society demand revolutionary democracy. More dangerous is to have the form without the substance.

Experience in the newly independent countries teaches us that a national bourgeoisie can arise in various ways. It can develop from land owing, large scale farming, various branches of merchandising, manufacturing, and speculation. In many cases, privileges from the system—or more rarely, high efficiency—permits rapid and unusual expansion of the business into profitable proportions. Practice of the professions, especially legal service to important imperialist firms or enterprises, can lead to the development of a native bourgeoisie. There is also at least one case in Guyana of private high school operation leading to the development of the national bourgeoisie. This is the well known case of JC Luck[2], where the business of this high school had to be managed on capitalist lines.

The position of the political elite in the poor countries must now be examined. In the countries in which the people are conscious of an experience of struggle, the political elite can come to power, or to office, no other way than under the banner of reform of the corrupt colonial administrations, national liberation and economic revolution. Sometimes they promise what is beyond their capacity, and that of the country, in the short run. At whatever pitch their ideology might be—high or low—without a doubt, they present themselves as friends of the people, as being at one with the people, as allies of the people against the enemy. However, the political elite is most often working on those models of living that were maintained by the high colonial

---

2   JC Luck was the founder of "Central High School," at one time the largest private secondary school in Guyana. -ed.

officials. The new rulers, as was said, except for their public positions and political slogans, are carbon copies of the old colonial officials. They differ verbally, but not inwardly. Their dream of the good life, of what it is important to achieve personally is very little different, in most cases, from what the agents of colonial oppression wished to achieve. Like any philistine in the community, the members of the political elite see their progress in terms of mansions, property, exclusive looking cars, and bank accounts. They use their pre-eminence in the community to take command of credit as a vehicle to other things for which they dearly dream. In many cases, taking into account also the lapse of time, they have outdone the colonial officials by a long way.

A choice they should make is between the love of the people and the lap of luxury. They should realize that if they wish to be of permanent use to their people, they must renounce all those material fetishes and false gods that put a gap between them and the people. If they have faith in whatever new system they claim to be building, they must not suffer from the insecurity that makes men avaricious and grasping; for the moment this stage is reached, the nature of the revolution changes and the people become their slaves. They cannot have, for long, both the love of the poorest sections of the people and the companionship of a living which is luxurious by comparison. Africans should study the systems of Shaka, Nyerere and Sekou Toure for inspiration, The Indians have well known examples.

It does not help when the parties are tied to Eastern European socialism. The political elite of Eastern Europe are not philosophers. They live by the law of consumption and oppose abstention. Marx would be surprised to see them caught up in the fetishism of commodities. In Europe, power is understood in terms of mansions and palaces, hardware, command over armies, and the right to decide or take instructions without consultation. The Europeans now alive have always been accustomed to a ruling, that is, a dominating class of their own kith and kin. If the Communist Party take over, and its leaders occupy the same gilded halls of presidential palaces, the effect of their power is very rapidly seen in the liquidation of the bourgeoisie. At any rate, some of those old palaces are given over to the people as museums, schools, libraries or palaces of culture. The difference is that in succeeding the bourgeoisie in their own European country, the revolutionaries are still on very good national soil and, in setting up a ruling elite with privileges, they are following national traditions.

Even so, the original Soviet discipline was extremely severe on members of the Communist Party, as reported by Sidney and Beatrice Webb and others. I am not up to date on the lifestyle of the elite in the various socialist countries. Reports about recent trends are conflicting. If our Western Hemisphere Marxists wish to copy from Europe they should copy the old guard Leninists who, although exercising state power very effectively, were schooled in the example of simple living and self sacrifice by the extraordinary half Mongolian.[3] Rather, our compatriots spread stories of how a famous European Communist, when asked why he liked to eat in luxurious restaurants, said that he had nowhere read in Marx that revolutionaries were not to eat in luxurious restaurants!

The fact of the people's response to leaders who become more and more caught up in the commodity worship living is not unknown in the West Indies. There is a story of a Minister of Education in an independent West Indian country, who was observed driving a car which seemed to have everything wrong—

---

3   While historical accounts of the Russian Revolution generally have yet to question the ascetic personality of Lenin, radicals today should be open to inquiring what the meaning of "effective exercise" of state power by the Bolsheviks was in regard to workers' autonomy. See, for example: Maurice Brinton. (1970) *The Bolsheviks and Workers' Control, 1917-1921: The State and Counter-Revolution.* Atlanta: On Our Own Authority! Publishing, 2012; GP Maximoff. (1940) *The Guillotine at Work: The Leninist Counter-Revolution.* Chicago: Cienfuegos Press, 1979. -ed.

bad fenders, broken windows, everything. When he was asked by friends to explain the style, he remarked, "Well, you see elections are coming and I can't afford to let the people think I am wealthy." The lifestyle being discussed is therefore not the "simple life" of a miser, or of a rich man who is concealing his wealth, so as "not to be considered wealthy" by the public. It is that of the members of the political elite and the cultural elite—if there is one—imposing rigid standards on themselves or accepting standards imposed by their party, limiting their wealth. It must be rooted in limitation of income.

A political worker who is too poor to buy people, and who sees himself in leadership functions—or has them thrust upon him—must, if he is not rich or wealthy by comparison, rely on spiritual and moral qualities, and on the quality of his activity, and his work, to keep the goodwill of the group, community, or country in which he works.

A serious cultural point must now be made. The African thinkers have always claimed that Africa's main contribution to the world is spiritual, rather than material. The Indians (Hindus) have made a similar claim. We are people who have sprung from those origins; and those who are still sane are not impressed by the trappings of power, but by the moral or spiritual values that should be typical of those who hold power. What we expected to help our political and government organs to build is a community of equals and not a society of new extortioners.

The old classical bourgeoisie had its well known method and structure of exploitation. They invested money, and having done this, lived royally off their investments and exploitation. Marx exposed the law of capitalist exploitation, in which the capitalist seizes the "surplus value" created by the workers' labor power and compensates the worker with wages, the price of which is below the value that the worker had created. In course of time, as Engels admitted, the details of capitalist exploitation changed, and the product became the product of "a series of capitals" and of labor itself. The principle of exploitation remained and will live as capitalism itself. The role of investor, however, has become quite important in the modern capitalist world. It has become an international interest, seeking guarantees and succeeding in obtaining legislation to protect it. In a big company, only the really big investor is a decision maker; the smaller ones are their front men, their propagandists and advocates. This type of capitalist is, of course, being reproduced daily in all societies in which they are free to develop. In particular, they are developing and carrying on the work of reproduction in the Caribbean, though their multiplication is not very rapid.

In African experience literature, the exploitation of public resources by individual politicians or administrators is called "eating" or "chopping." "He chop, make I chop," is a very popular phrase among Africans who are describing a system of corruption.[4]

The bourgeoisie, often arising from among the political elite, have an investors' attitude to the public resources. Their attitude is that they have done so much for the people that anything they take from the public resources is an insufficient reward for their works of salvation. These acts of salvation can never be adequately paid back. In some places, just as investors look for continual dividends from their investments, so do some members of the political elite demand unending tribute for their services. No doubt, they employ funds from the public resources to insure against loss of political office, and therefore show that they are stuck amidst the rocks of insecurity.

The question of ideology, not as a badge to be flaunted, but as a world outlook with a way of life attached, is important in relation to the April crisis, in relation to any other crisis, and in relation to everyday work. It is for this reason that point is made the

---

4   This is especially so in West Africa, particularly in Ghana. -ed.

after-gaff.

What is lifestyle is not merely a question of whether or not one wears expensive clothes, or drives a cheap car instead of a reasonably priced one. It is not merely a question of living so as not to "offend" supporters with the exhibition of grandeur. It is all of those, and it is chiefly a way of thinking and living.

Exploitation of man by man does not disappear with capitalism, just as it did not start with capitalism. It does not disappear with nationalization. If a small group is living extremely well, within a sector, at the expense of the humbler workers, exploitation may be present. The surplus value is then not seized by capitalist investors, but by people of the investor mentality who, because they have the power to decide things, can, without owning shares, exploit the work force. This point has been made of the ruling elite in certain Socialist Republics of Europe. Serious political leaders will, therefore, rely heavily on the vigilance of the people, and will allow public critical investigation of their actions by observers. If leading groups are committed and truly egalitarian in word and intention, mistakes in their actions will be quickly corrected and not become habits. This way the leadership can win and ought to have a very strong moral position among the people. Again, on this vital question of lifestyle, we must remember the age-old indoctrination of all our people by Europe, with their outmoded values.

At those stages of economic revolution, when we still talk of sacrifices, and call on the people to make them, the lifestyle of the leadership must be one of abstinence from wealth. Especially at a time when the law insures a minister, as much as it can, against the state of a pauper by providing pensions. If the leader groups preach sacrifice, and practice accumulation and self enrichment, the morale of the movement will go to pieces. The leading groups will not help matters if, in trying to deal with the people's counterattack, they point to, or examine, not themselves, but "the imperialists". True, the imperialists are the most guilty, because it is their standards that our new leaders may be trying feverishly to copy. Yet, the political elite in these countries are very flexible, not deep-seated or deep-rooted, and is capable of reform under certain conditions.

This little work does not set out to explain ASCRIA's ideology, its political position, or to give its views on every possible issue. It is simply the application of our way of thinking, our ideology to aspects of a given industrial explosion in the bauxite industry after the decision to nationalize was taken by the Guyana government. The after gaff turns attention to some of the political needs of leadership in the Caribbean, and the First World generally. Many of the questions in the minds of *ndugu*, brothers and sisters and comrades, about our general position on various points will be reexamined in a second edition of *Teachings of the Cultural Revolution* after the new draft has been examined by the Council of Elders, the Council of Captains, the ideological classes, and the Ujamaa School.

Chapter Seven:
Leaflets

In the following pages, many of the leaflets issued at Linden during the April strike are reprinted. Those headed *Voice Of The Workers* were issued by the strikers' organization. Those headed "The Voice of the Real Workers" were issued by the Peoples National Congress. There are two issued by ASCRIA, one of them going back as far as 1970, the time of the nurses' strike. In between leaflets are a few reprints from the daily press.

The leaflets showed the development of a very active workers and citizens' democracy. They are reprinted here because they show that history is not made by a few people making speeches and writing books, or by national assemblies of government and opposition. The bodies with the power of compulsion have the ability to support or oppose, assist or divert to later times, an historical trend. Seldom have they done much more.

These leaflets are published because whether or not they bear out the argument of this book, they show groups of people in the situation speaking for themselves and society out of that situation.

One very interesting feature is that nowhere did the GMWU enter into the leaflet agitation. Another is that the PNC was forced to enter into it and for a time use a form of struggle demanded by events.

It is interesting to watch the positions develop. All of this helps all of us to learn to govern. My commentary is one point of view. After this book is read many insights on the life we are trying to build will be expressed by comrades, brothers and sisters in many places. The prints also help us to capture the mood of the hot fortnight.

There are some attitudes of the revolt that are extremely

narrow. There is no evidence that they rejected, not for the elite, but for themselves the concept of the life style lived by elite. But the revolt reaches it climax when on May 20, 1971 it cried out: "Retrenchment is a word that drives fear into the hearts of every worker. Less over all increase and no retrenchment ever, ever, is the kind of assurance for security of our future we want."

This is an excellent basis for the solution of one of the most vicious problems of the working people. This common bond, this unwillingness to progress at the expense of the brother is an important aspect of the new social morality.

The new Leadership role of Chase Manhattan Bank, as opposed to the Royal Bank of Canada, in the oligarchy of expatriate Banks; the declaration that the Commercial banks will not be nationalized but controlled; the flight from 'miniaturization'; the continued interest of the USA in financing our road development and infrastructure the embracing of China, and Maha Saba but the alienation or rejection of ASCRIA, an anti-imperialist organization; these trends do not call for the callous accusation of people but for keen study by our citizens.

Imperialist desire for a crisis in April 1971 would not be satisfied if the institutions had not been out dated: The strikers were emphatically not agents of DEMBA. They felt they had an urgent cause to fight just when ALCAN most wanted a crisis.

If the crisis had been nipped in the bud, the government would be in a stronger position in deciding the amount and terms of payment for the bauxite assets. ALCAN exploited the fact that the labor force was restive and the government was not in touch with the situation.

Mr. Carrington's statement made on April 19th and afterward, printed on a signed leaflet, was the basis of the final settlement. But it ran foul of the strikers' desire to see the Prime Minister. It caused the ASCRIA compound and dozens of workers to go back to work.

Note too that the strikers did not use the opportunities open to them to deepen the crisis. Apart from making threats when they began to doubt the outcome, they used their power with restraint.

The professional politicians should remember: when leadership passes out of your hands it is not the fault of those who take over. First, examine your own attitude inside out.

The demand by the Committee of ten "Workers participation is a must" is another high point of the revolt. Many workers correctly shy away from any part in the decision making process under capitalism, because then it is a trick to prolong capitalism by 'involving' workers. But in a firm without private owners, there is no reason why workers involvement should be delayed.

"Complete Shutdown at Linden"
(*Guyana Graphic*: Wednesday, April 21, 1971.)

The Labour Minister told a meeting late yesterday, at which Mr. Eusi Kwayana was present, that his Ministry was prepared to call on the arbitrator to make the monetary award (wages) now, so as to satisfy the workers' demand for relief.

He told them that the non-monetary issues before the Tribunal could then be dealt with later. The Minister told the strikers that the payout of the award should take two weeks.

Mr. Carrington explained that, because of the delay, the government had suggested to DEMBA that an interim payment could be made to workers, but the company turned down the proposal and said it was prepared to await the findings of the Tribunal.

The Minister stressed to the strikers that when the Prime Minister issues his instructions government will see to it that the company carries out its obligations by a fixed date. About 250 workers were at the meeting.

Strikers' Leaflet
(22nd April 1972.)

We the workers have stated our stand to the press, radio, government, the Hon. Minister of Labor and the Leader of the Opposition.

This is no political issue, but a bread and butter one. It is an industrial one.

We are demanding that the Tyndal Tribunal's Report be made public. We are of the view that only the intervention of the Prime Minister of Guyana can solve this problem. That is why we invited the Leader of the Opposition to Mackenzie to impress upon the Prime Minister the severity of the situation and to see that he uses his influence to resolve this crisis.

We take note that a band of renegades who are misguiding the Prime Minister and the public have declared themselves a "New Action Committee" and have promised to offer leadership to the workers who they claim are leaderless. We are not interested in leadership at this time. We did not appoint anyone to represent us at no time, and no place.

Our demands are the same as regards to the Prime Minister, etc.

"DEMBA STRIKE"
(Editorial, *Evening Post*: THURSDAY, April 22, 1971.)

Reports coming from Linden about the DEMBA strike are not, at the time of writing, quite clear; but to all appearances, while the situation is by no means out of hand, it holds rather anxious moments for the government at this stage of the takeover arrangements.

For once, perhaps, in the history of the company, management seems unconcerned over the results of the strike and has turned down a proposal from Minister of Labor Winslow Carrington for an interim payout to the workers, pending a report on the findings of the Tyndall Tribunal established last October to settle the question of wage increases.

It would seem to suit the purpose of management to cause as much embarrassment to the government by refusing to build confidence in the workers that their benefits will be assured under nationalization. And this the workers ought to bear in mind-that in resorting to the kind of action they are reported to have taken, they are unwittingly playing into the hands of management.

It should not be forgotten that it was recently reported that ALCAN is of the opinion that the doors for negotiation on meaningful participation are still open.

For our part, we will not at all be surprised to learn that elements sympathetic to the cause of ALCAN have incited the strike. Behind it there is an atmosphere of confusion which casts grave doubts as to whether workers have a single purpose behind the shutdown. While some appear to be calling for the payout of the RILA fund, others are calling for the publication of the findings of the Tyndall Tribunal and others still seem to be annoyed with the union executive for the kind of representation being made which, they claim, is delaying the work of the arbitration tribunal.

In this confused state of mind the situation can easily explode and the duty devolves itself on all those who exercise some influence over the workers to explain the true position to them. In this connection, the presence of Coordinating Elder of ASCRIA, Mr. Eusi Kwayana, at Linden, on Tuesday, is reassuring.

"The Return of Dr. Jagan"
(Editorial, *Evening Post*: Friday, April 23, 1971.)

After more than six years, opposition leader Dr. Cheddi Jagan, the man whose wife at the close of the last general elections claimed that the PPP leaders could not set foot in the Mackenzie area for fear of losing their lives, returned to the district at the invitation of union members to advise on the DEMBA strike dispute.

It was an opportunity which, for political reasons, Dr. Jagan could not afford to miss. And it is to be hoped that the reception given him is a happy augury of return to racial and political peace in the area.

The next few days will tell; for already a section of the union has voiced its disapproval of the action taken by those who issued the invitation to Dr. Jagan, and that in itself is ground for uneasiness over possible developments.

For ourselves, we can only see the invitation to the PPP leader as a sort of warning to Prime Minister Burnham that if he would not listen to the workers, there were those in the union who were prepared to have Dr. Jagan listen to them, for it has been reported that the workers have been asking Mr. Burnham, for some time now, to travel to Linden and explain the position on the different issues to them. They want to be informed at the highest level.

That being so, the invitation to Dr. Jagan to intervene in the matter was an exercise in futility—born of frustration, yes; but absolutely senseless from the point of view of getting Dr. Jagan to make conclusions.

And as a matter of fact, no one seemed to appreciate this point better than Dr. Jagan himself, though he used the opportunity afforded him to advise the workers to keep the RILA funds out of a government created trust and to insist that DEMBA should hand over to them all of its contributions made on their behalf.

In saying this, Dr. Jagan could create a toe hole for himself in the workers' affection; so he certainly used his short return to the area to political advantage by making it somewhat more difficult for the government to appease the workers over the handling of the RILA funds.

"No Man Can Serve Two Masters"
(Community Relations Dept. ASCRIA – Wismar Compound, Linden April 23rd, 1970.)

For nearly one week, we have been out on strike and for the duration of that period, ASCRIA-Wismar Compound looked on with interest at what took place. Everyone was allowed to act out their chosen roles. We said nothing. But we feel that this confounded nonsense must now be brought to an end.

We do not deny that there is genuine cause for discontent among the workers. And, though we knew that any strike at this moment would be misrepresented on the International Political scene, we nevertheless came out voluntarily with our striking brothers and sisters. We believe in solid industrial unity.

But it should be quite clear by now to any reasonable individual, that the workers have been misled, misguided and misused by a few persons whose ambitions—it seems—are beyond industrial achievement. They tell us that this is a bread and butter struggle, but all they have achieved for us so far is a loss of this said bread and butter.

They claim that they are against political influence in the union, and that this is strictly an industrial struggle. They warn us against PNC control, and yet they sell us out to the PPP. They criticise the Prime Minister, but we would like to ask them who it was that ruled the Country in the days of the Son Chapman tragedy, when numerous black bodies floated and rotted in the river because of the evil design of their new-found friends. And who ruled Guyana when our brothers and sisters were raped and slaughtered along the East and West Coast Demerara and in the Mahaicony Creek and other areas? Have we forgotten so quickly?

If this was indeed an industrial struggle, it should have been brought to an end on the advice and promise of the Minister of Labour, given under his signature, that the monetary aspects of Tribunal Award must be made in two weeks. The Minister of Labour is the final competent authority on industrial matters, not Jagan.

This whole rotten affair developed as a direct consequence of the subtle maneuvering Imperialist Forces and their local lackeys and a genuine workers' grouse' was twisted into a big Political Power Game.

A very important question should be answered by any intelligent person.

They claim the Prime Minister slammed his phone during a conversation asking for his presence. This is what happened: They phoned the Prime Minister saying "You have until twelve o'clock to be here or else..."

Let us ask ourselves, "Can any worker speak to his foremen or supervisor in this manner?" This is the Prime Minister of independent Guyana they were talking to. Apparently these self-styled leaders have no respect for authority, much more the Prime Minister.

We could not have done it to our colonial masters, why then should we do it to our national leader?

The Union Leadership is dead. Those who misguided the workers are dying rapidly. DEMBA is having a big laugh, and Jagan was allowed a foothold in our community which Burnham would have never been allowed in Port Mourant.

We are resuming work today, and no one will dare harm us. We give the workers this assurance.

Voice of the Workers
(Guyana Mine Workers Hall: April 23rd, 1970)

Comrades,

Wismar Compound ASCRIA has once more seen it proper to air the opportunistic designs for leadership of the *Bauxite Workers*. The workers of DEMBA once held Burgess Huntley Pro for ASCRIA – Wismar Compound in their confidence. This confidence was demonstrated beyond any doubt when they elected him to represent them.

It is well known that ASCRIA claims to make the African people aware of their culture; there is no quarrel with this. Huntley, at the time he was secretary of the Industrial Branch, got the support of all of the workers of DEMBA, *Indians, Africans, Chinese and Amerindians*; because he represented them in their struggle for bread and butter. There is no racial connections to the struggle for bread and butter. All are involved.

ASCRIA's newsletter has very strong and disturbing *racial* tendencies and this will do damage to the peaceful progress more than any action taken by the workers of Guyana and indeed undermines the Prime Minister's efforts to have unity and peace among all the peoples of Guyana; so that we may be a progressive nation.

We are quite certain that ASCRIA's newsletter cannot help us in this struggle for bread and butter. *Only the united and determined* efforts can win through. We all remembered, when we went on strike in support of the nurses, how ASCRIA defied the call for resumption of work and caused that strike to prolong. Did not ASCRIA cause a loss of bread and butter? Now they say that we are losing bread and butter because we have come out on strike for what is just.

ASCRIA is well aware that the workers of DEMBA have *no confidence* in the Minister of Labor and should remember that the

Minister of Labor presided at the talks for a resumption of work in the nurses issue, which Mr. Burgess Huntley was present as a secretary of the Industrial Branch.

He later said that all of the Union's representatives, and the Minister of Labor, were drunk and it is well known that Mr. Huntley does not drink, yet he, Huntley, signed the agreement.

Our request for the Prime Minister to come to us is not a sin of disloyalty to him. This shows that since we, as workers, are leaderless and have no confidence in the Minister of Labor, and call on the PM. This request displays that we recognize that only he can solve our problems and this alone is a sign of undisguised *loyalty and confidence* in the Prime Minister.

Dr. Jagan's coming here happened only because the PM did not come, and we make no apologies for this. ASCRIA's newsletter is designed to create very serious *racial* problems once again in Guyana.

We call on ASCRIA's coordinating elder, Mr. Eusi Kwayana, to take firm action against ASCRIA's Wismar Compound, which is no doubt out to break a very serious racial problem for the country.

We know very well that the views on the newsletter are not shared by every member of ASCRIA. We know that the union's leadership is dead and when it comes to that, we shall solve it.

Our request remains the same: that the Prime Minister come to Linden to solve our problem or we *SHALL NOT WORK*.

PM Says: DEMBA is Anti-National
(*Sunday Graphic*: April 24, 1971)

On Monday, 1st March 1971, the Parliament of Guyana, by the overwhelming majority of forty-eight votes to three, passed the Bauxite Nationalization Act. This Act empowers the government to nationalize the Demerara Bauxite Company and, in spite of what the Aluminum Company of Canada, their subsidiary DEMBA,

116

or their agents may say or think, there is no turning back. There is absolutely no question of ALCAN or its subsidiary participating in the ownership, control or operation of the Bauxite Industry in Guyana.

Since the passing of the Bauxite Nationalization Act, it has become evident that DEMBA and its agents have deliberately set out on a policy of confusing the workers at Linden, and have, it appears, in some measure, succeeded in doing so, especially on the question of the award to be made by the Tyndall Tribunal.

It will be recalled that on Saturday, 17th October, 1970, when the Guyana Mine Workers' Union and the Demerara Bauxite Company failed to reach agreement after 12 months of meetings, on the question of employment, I intervened personally in the interest of the workers. I intimated to the management of DEMBA, who had refused to go to arbitration, that unless they agreed to arbitration of the outstanding issues, my government would have introduced legislation making arbitration compulsory.

As a result of my intervention, on Monday, 19th October, 1970, DEMBA agreed to the arbitration for which the Mine Workers' Union had been pressing. On the 18th November, 1970, the Arbitration Tribunal was appointed. The Tribunal comprised Mr. Joseph Tyndall, who headed it, and Messrs. John Durey and Neville Griffith, nominated respectively by the workers.

The Arbitration Tribunal has now completed its hearings. The formal hearings covered 35 meetings and over 105 hours. The Tribunal is at present considering the evidence and submissions of both sides which involves over 1000 pages and, in addition, 80 documentary exhibits.

I have already stated, and it should be pellucidly clear, that, whatever is the award of the Tribunal; the new wages, the vacation pay and payment of the national holiday Youman Naubi will be retroactive to 2nd February, 1970, the date of expiry of the previous Company/Union Agreement. I emphasized then, that DEM-

BA, irrespective of what its agents may now say, would be under compulsion to honor the award of the Tribunal. I repeat now that DEMBA is still under compulsion to honor the award in respect of all retroactive payment and up to and until Vesting Day and government undertakes to honor the award from Vesting Day.

I do not envisage the Demerara Bauxite Company refusing to honor the Tribunal's award, but if perchance the company should attempt to do so, let me make it clear that the government is in a position to enforce payment, for DEMBA will still have assets remaining in Guyana subject to government confiscation.

It ought to be understood that in the circumstances, whether the Tribunal's award is made before or after Vesting Day is immaterial, in so far as the workers' benefits are concerned. Any statement or suggestion, from whatever source, to the contrary is therefore intended and calculated to turn the workers at Linden and the people of Guyana against the nationalization of DEMBA, which has already been decided upon by government.

The present behavior of DEMBA can only be regarded as antinational. It is reminiscent of the machinations of the Anglo-Iranian Oil Company in Persia in 1951 when the Persian government had nationalized the Oil Industry. The Aluminum Company of Canada, it appears, is determined to make a last ditch stand. This we must expect from those who have exploited our resources in the past almost exclusively for their own benefit and who, it seems, will stop at nothing to keep us as their economic slaves.

Some concern has also been expressed in regard to the question of the workers' pension and assurance rights, at present covered by the Mean Retirement Income and Life Assurance Plan (RILA). Immediately upon the workers at Linden returning to work, the government shall submit for their information, examination and comment firm proposals with respect to the establishment of a new pension scheme. Immediate arrangements will be made for government to receive, at Linden, the views of the workers' representative on this question.

I have held discussions with Mr. Joseph Tyndall, Chairman of the Arbitration Tribunal, and I have been assured by him that the Tribunal will be in a position to make its findings known within three weeks though it will, however, take some time longer for the full report to be submitted.

As soon as the Tribunal's findings are made known—i.e. within three weeks—they will be acted upon.

(Office of the Prime Minister, April 24, 1971.)

PRESS REPORT :

"Four Ministers go to Linden"
(*Guyana Graphic*: Friday, April 30, 1971.)

The situation in the strike-torn town of Linden remained grim yesterday, as the bulk of the workers remained outside demonstrating, talking and demanding the payment of the Tyndall Arbitration Tribunal Award before Vesting Day.

Last night the strikers passed a series of resolutions calling upon the government to investigate the financial position of the Guyana Mine Workers' Union. They banned the GMWU executive and Labour Minister, Winslow Carrington, from entering the Wismar Street Office of the union at Mackenzie.

They also demanded the immediate release of the men who were refused bail on Wednesday and remanded to prison, and stated that this was one of the conditions for a resumption of work.

These resolutions were made known to a team of government Ministers, led by Deputy Prime Minister Dr. Ptolemy Reid, who, since arriving in the town at midnight Wednesday, has been meeting strikers and urging them to end the 11-day strike.

Dr. Reid, whose team went up as a result of a Cabinet decision, spent over two hours with the strikers at the union hall early yesterday telling them that it was in their interest and in the interest of the country and the government that they should keep the bauxite plants rolling.

Later on, the Minister assured the strikers that the Prime Minister would keep his promise to have the awards paid out immediately after the Tyndall Arbitration Tribunal released its report.

Speaking to a large group of the strikers outside the main gate of the bauxite plant just before the 7am horn was sounded yesterday, Dr. Reid told the workers: "The PM has not let down the sugar workers. Would he let you down?"

He urged the strikers to put their trust and confidence in their government and in the Prime Minister.

But most of the strikers said that they had made arrangements for Dr. Reid to meet and address them at the union hall at 11pm.

Dr. Reid, however said that the time was not convenient and would have his conversation with them right there.

Some of the strikers left, and while a group of 14 marched up and down with slogans—bearing placards. Dr. Reid said: "I am certain that when you return to work, the Prime Minister will come here. But I cannot see, in any circumstances, the Prime Minister coming here because of an order given by some of the people at Mackenzie."

"You have made it extremely difficult for the Prime Minister," Dr. Reid declared.

After the strikers referred to police action on the previous day, Dr. Reid told them that whatever happened at Mackenzie was because of what the strikers had done.

"If your children are gassed, it is because of you. If you are brutalized by the police, it is because of you. Once you are idle, all sorts of things will happen. One thing is certain, this government will maintain law and order. It is disgusting, as far as I am concerned, to see things like this happen."

After the Deputy Prime Minister had spoken, there was a brief but heated discussion between Ministers Hubert Jack and Hamilton Green on one side and the strikers on the other. The strikers called on the Ministers to meet them at their union hall and eventually the Ministers moved over to the union hall.

By this time though, only a small percentage of workers had gone into the mills.

Reports said about twenty-five percent of the industrial force was out at work yesterday. But this did not reflect in the productivity rate. Most of the mines are in operation, and there are many cars in which to transport the ore. Most of the locomotive drivers are on strike.

Hundreds of wives and mothers, as well as school children, were out in the streets demonstrating and carrying slogans with words like: "We don't want guns, we want money."

Mr. Hubert Jack told a large gathering at the union hall that as Minister charged with the responsibility of naming "Vesting Day," he was giving the assurance that he had not yet done so.

In response to calls from within the gathering, Mr. Jack said: "You must understand there are certain things in nature of risings I cannot say here. But you can be assured that I am conscious of your concern and I have the ultimate decision to make in naming "Vesting Day".

Despite these assurances, the corps of spokesmen who have come forward since the main strike leaders were incarcerated that Wednesday, declared that they would remain on strike until they have been given a definite undertaking that they would receive their retroactive pay a definite date before Vesting Day.

Another spokesman said that they did not want to see DEMBA pull out of Guyana before they were in receipt of retroactive pay.

And another appealed: "In the interest of peace, just give us the assurance that we are going to get our money before Vesting-Day."

The theme of all the speakers including women workers and housewives, was: "We want our money before a resumption of work."

The strikers also passed another resolution recalling incidents at union hall on Wednesday which they say caused a worker to be hospitalized because of injuries inflicted by a policeman.

They said that the workers at DEMBA do not receive free hospital benefits. There the injured worker should be paid compensation for earnings lost that he should also be remunerated for his hospital expenses.

There was a mild uproar at the union hall when Mr. Hamilton Green, Minister of Works, and Hydraulics and Supply addressed the workers. (From Eleazer Watson at Linden)

ASCRIA Statement
(*Evening Post:* Thursday, May 6, 1971.)

"The authorities will be well advised to investigate and have the charges against the Linden strikers withdrawn, as a step to restoring normal conditions in the area," says the African Society for Cultural Relations with Independent Africa (ASCRIA).

It is clear that whoever was responsible made mistakes. These should be corrected without delay. The covering up of blunders and blunderers is not in keeping with a serious approach to nationalization of DEMBA.

SOLIDARITY

"Rather, complete solidarity of the workers of every mood and level of consciousness is needed. Even from a non-partisan and strictly industrial point of view, everything must be done to restore community solidarity and to prevent fragmentation of the labor force at Linden."

And Coordinating Elder Eusi Kwayana has stated:

"In my personal opinion, the Prime Minister is not getting the advice he deserves from most of his advisers. Saying this in public may affect our very good relationship, but there are bigger things than this relationship. We cannot see a well-intentioned man who is trying to do everything that ought to be done—challenging imperialism in a concrete way—we cannot see such a man messed up in the way he is now being messed up.

"Some of the Prime Minister's advisers want to make him a prime minister after their own image, a kind of rubber stamp. In effect, they want to separate him from the people. This will be a crime, because he is all the people have left in the former colonial West Indies."

Asked to be more specific, Mr. Kwayana said the comments applied to the administration, the Cabinet and the Party. "Everything points to a lack of common attitude. People whose skins have ceased to feel should be discarded.

"Too many of them are concerned with status, with prestige, with power, with rivalry and other things that don't matter. Many have no ideology, no compass for their actions…"

Voice of the Workers
(May 19th, 1971)

The workers of GMWU do not care to follow Verbeke and others into this new era-entity, we have too much too lose. Essentially the trouble which faces us today has been created by those who seek to destroy the free trade union movement as a means of exploiting our union funds constitutionally. What we have to receive from the Tyndell Arbitration award did not need or worth bargaining for [sic]; yet we had to strike for fourteen days in order that those who intend to exploit us would understand that we will no longer tolerate this." We cannot have political puppets at the bead of our Union to bargain for us with a government. We are saying that we want a Union free from all political interference," We have ourselves and our families to look after. Our trade union loyalty must come first, then our political loyalty after. In simpler words—ourselves first, then any other thing after. This is not being selfish—this is nature's first law. This is bread and butter."

The TUC keeps stressing over the years that the workers must have representatives of their own choice. We will not allow Verbeke and others to force themselves on us. This is supposed to be a free democratic country and as such we must have freedom of choice. We have absolutely no confidence in the Union Executive and Branch Officials of the GMWU We want free election and Verbeke and others must no longer be eligible to run for office.

In the best interest of industrial peace and progress we the workers are calling all responsible Guyanese to support us in our struggle for Free Trade Union Movement.

Voice of the Workers
(May 20th, 1971.)

The workers of the Demerara Bauxite Company are now inspecting the Tyndall Arbitration award. Strict attention is being paid to the retrenchment benefits which have been increased favorably. We are saying that during the last month we have been fearful and absolutely dissatisfied over the sinister attitude of the government. With this new entity, we want more security than ever. Retrenchment is a word that drives fear into the hearts of every worker. Less over-all increase and no retrenchment ever, ever: this is the kind of assurance for the security of our future that we want. Workers who were here during the last big retrenchment in the early sixties would recall the living death-like atmosphere which came over Mackenzie: Everyday was like a Sunday. They would recall the sufferings in homes, the inevitable circumstance in which vandalism and crime strive. We hope that those days are gone forever. The mention of benefits for retrenchment is another injection from a big needle marked **FEAR.**

We still wish to be identified as nationals and do pledge our support to the government at this time. But there are certain things which bother us and we must voice them now.

Workers fear things like wage freezes and possible reduction of our present salary; imprompt payments for our labor; political appointees and victimization; finally political infiltration of our union.

On the other hand, we were expecting to receive from the award things like production target bonuses; triple pay for holidays; education benefits; hospitalization benefits; Bereavement leave with pay and finally, better loans for housing.

How can we feel that we are working with ourselves when we are still eating crumbs? We have not gotten any money yet and already the cost of living is going up. **Watch it.**

Voice of the Workers
(May 20th, 1971)

At a meet held at the GMWU Hall - Linden, workers of the Industrial, Clerical, Technical and Medical branches heard a report by the Workers' Committee on the legal steps to be taken towards the removal of Branch and Central Executives of the GMWU from the office.

The members present were brought up-to-date with the position of negotiations between the Demerara Bauxite Company and deep concern over the attitude of their branch officials with regards to their negotiations and stated that they are not aware of what is going on presently. However, the industrial workers pledged their support to their other comrades in their struggle to secure the monies and other benefits before Vesting Day.

This release wishes to bring attention to part of a statement made by Mr. Philbert Benjamin on May 17, 1971 in which he asked the workers to vacate our Union Building, etc.,etc...

The workers wish to point out that they have not banned these men from the Union Building; after all, we pay them and until such time as they are no longer in the employ of the workers they are free to do their job.

But we warned that any attempt by Branch and Central Officers to look-out or in any way deny the workers the right to use or occupy their union building will be met with the most vigorous resistance imaginable.

N.B. There will be a meeting today for workers of all Branches at the GMWU Hall.

"THE STRIKE CONTINUES"
(*Voice of the Workers:* May 21st, 1971)

Last night at a meeting at the GMWU Hall, the workers of the Clerical and Technical Branch decided to go on strike at 7:30 a.m. Today. The workers are demanding written commitment from DEMBA giving them the assurance that they will receive their retroactive monies at the same time as the industrial workers. They are also demanding that negotiations continue afterward for a better Collective Labor Agreement. These negotiations take time. The first one took fifteen months and the Company is rushing this one to have it completed in five days.

Workers are prepared to accept their retroactive monies on

the basis of the Tyndall Arbitration Award. The company is not prepared to pay the Clerical and Technical workers until their entire agreement is completed. The workers regard this as a bitter attempt to deprive or rob them of better fringes and better working facilities.

The workers do not intend to hold the fact that they have to pay out the awards to the Industrial branch as a ransom. Their brothers have already pledged their full support in this struggle. The Company should already know by now that workers solidarity is existing. The workers demands must be met before there is another complete shut-down of the Linden works. The government's attitude towards this situation leaves much to be desired.

In the best interest of Industrial Peace and the economy of the country, the workers insist that the government intervene effectively and immediately. **The Strike Continues.**

"VOICE OF THE WORKERS"
(May 24th, 1971)

A new era has dawned at Linden. Time has changed its dimension. The old order must change yielding place to new, least one bad custom should corrupt the entire of Guyana.

We, the workers, won the first phase of the struggle with the philosophy: **"Every man is his own leader, and we are leaderless."** The fact that we were never active and showed no interest in our union affairs created this grave situation. Now we must partake at all levels **meaningfully.** This must not happen only in our union, but also in our local authority and the new entity. At this time, our new philosophy is **"Worker's participation must be a must."** Why should we continue to allow other people to sit back and make decisions—good or bad—for us? We know exactly what we want. Our voice must be heard. Worker's involvement must be maximum.

Our voice is saying: Out with Verbeke, the entire Executive and Branch Officials." Our demands are "early elections" in which renegades must not be eligible or allowed to run for office.

If the Everton Branch wishes to secede, doing so now, in itself, might be a blessing in disguise for us here. The fact is that we have to subsidise them. If they love Verbeke, they could have him and others with all pleasure; obviously he will not accept Presidential post of a union representing Everton Branch's contribution. What would happen to those out of everywhere allowance; fifteen months of real speedy bargaining; lovely cocktail delegates conference; grand seminars;... fat juicy loans; enormous telephone and transportation bills. What would happen to them? Surely 'Beke knows they can't make out with Everton's contributions alone. A Threat – refusing to bargain and resign with tear-filled eyes did force them, under those circumstances, to vote Confidence. This is a dirty, low trick to woo public sympathy. But we shall not be moved. We have absolutely **No Confidence** in them. It would appear that to ask them to resign is too much to do and too decent to expect. They are in so much trouble that they are even claiming our victory—the Tyndall Report declared. They are like rats snatching at straws in order to survive. The workers are alert and can think for themselves. We shall prove whatever charges we lay against them. Verbekeism has outlived its usefulness. Our voice must be heard.

THE VOICE OF THE REAL WORKERS

"Who is Playing with the Workers' Future ?"

(Peoples National Congress, Linden. May 28, 1971)

Very soon the new bauxite company will be a reality. The

GUYANA BAUXITE COMPANY LIMITED will be here to stay. DEMBA will be done for ever.

DEMBA is leaving reluctantly. No one gives up a good thing easily. Al CAN does nor intend to give up without a fight. ALCAN is determined to destroy GUYBAUX even before it has started—if they can.

ALCAN is playing politics with the workers' future and ALCAN has its local stooges masquerading as Guyanese workers to try and do it for them.

Your government, from that day on Saturday, November 8, 1970, when the Prime Minister announced he would negotiate for majority participation, has been fighting against Mean for what is rightfully ours.

Your government, since then has fought ALCAN outside of Guyana and, in spite of them, has won markets for bauxite, organized supplies for the operation, arranged the finance to run it and has retained the best of the top brains to work with us.

Now, ALCAN has turned its attention to Guyana. If Mean can divide us at home, if ALCAN stops us producing bauxite in Guyana. ALCAN has succeeded in destroying us even before we get started. ALCAN is now attempting, THROUGH ITS AGENTS AND STOOGES MASQUERADING AS WORKERS to subvert the loyalty of the Guyanese bauxite workers to the new company.

We have had one strike already. Many reasons were advanced to justify it. But who did it really hurt? Did it hurt DEMBA ? Did it hurt ALCAN ? No it did not. It hurt the workers and it hurt Guiana. Who did it really serve ? It served the interests of ALCAN. ALCAN now tell the rest of the world, to whom we have to sell our bauxite and alumina, that we are fighting among ourselves before we have even started. Would you sign a contract to buy products you need from an unreliable producer ?

Now pamphlets which are supposed to come from the GMWU are circulating fears of "retrenchment, reduction of salaries political appointees" etc. All this in the name of the " Voice of the Workers."

This is the voice of ALCAN speaking. This is the doctrine of fear and confusion that ALCAN has persuaded others to spread, either in their innocence or their ignorance.

Follow this "voice," have more strikes, continue to hold the people of Guyana up to ransom, go on stopping production and all we will succeed in doing is destroying OURSELVES.

That is what ALCAN wants to see.

Your Pension and Insurance Future.
The Decision is Yours. Make it Yourself...

(People's National Congress: May 25, 1971.)

Over the past two weeks the government Bauxite Development Unit together with an international actuary has spent some 16 hours discussing with the real workers the new pension and assurance plan to replace the RILA plan when the new nationally owned bauxite company takes over from DEMBA.

The government did not settle for a single meeting in a public square and then ask for a mandate. The government talked directly with the workers for 16 hours and *listened* to the workers views and *answered* the workers questions. *Constructive* criticism not *destructive*, was asked for and given. Compare this with emotional meetings full of empty speeches and decide who has our interests at heart. 'The voice of the workers' was peculiarly silent at these discussions., They asked no questions, offered no suggestions, said nothing constructive, but *The Voice Of The Real Workers* was there, was heard. They spoke for themselves.

Government Bauxite Development Unit made it plain. Our pension and assurance future is ours to decide, not as a group, but individuals. The government told us that each member of the

RILA plan would receive a letter explaining the option available to him or her. Attached to that letter will be a questionnaire giving each one of us *in the privacy of our own homes* the opportunity to decide and answer whether we wish to transfer our years of service in RILA to the new company's pension scheme or terminate now.

This is an important decision. Do we discuss it with our families, do we give it serious study and thought, or do we stand up in a public square and give a mandate to those who say they are our friends to decide for us?

We all know that if we terminate our membership in RILA now, thousands of dollars owed to the bauxite workers of Guyana will remain in Canada. We all should know that this in the end will benefit only ALCAN. Whether we are RILA members for less than twelve years, or whether we have 84 points, we all understand that we have much to gain and a lot to loose if we do not transfer to the new pension scheme.

We all know that the government has put the facts to us and have told us the decision is ours to make, as individuals. Why are others so keen to rush us into a decision by a show of hands in public? Whose interest do they really intend to serve? We have 5000 workers at Linden and Ituni. Can a few shouting at Cuffy Square decide for all of us? And those who want to railroad us now at public meetings, and claim to have a mandate, preach about "every man is his own leader."

Let every man decide for himself, in his own home, what he wants done with his pension money. Let every man wait for the government questionnaire and give his own answer. Nobody has a mandate to speak for us.

When the government questionnaires have been answered and handed back to the government, then and only then there will be a mandate and only for those who decide to give it. ALCAN will have to wait for that decision and ALCAN will have to abide by it.

The legitimate interests of the bauxite workers can only be represented by the written decision of each worker. What matters now is unity: unity with the Prime Minister, unity against ALCAN.

Beware the Voice of ALCAN in Disguise
(People's National Congress, Linden: May 30, 1971.)

The real workers at Linden and Ituni now have the responsibility of running the new nationally owned Guyana Bauxite Company. Ours is the responsibility of making for ourselves and the people of Guyana a success of the industry which we have taken control over.

If we succeed, we will reap the benefits. If we fail, we have ourselves to blame. Let us understand that ALCAN has a vested interest in our failure. One certain way of failing is to allow the agents of ALCAN to persuade us into closing down production.

Our first task is to learn to distinguish between those who are our friends and those who claim to be our friends, particularly "new found friends."

Our leader and Prime Minister, let us not forget it, got the Tyndall Tribunal set up in the first place when all else had failed. When the management of DEMBA refused to go to arbitration after 12 months of fruitless negotiation with the Union, it was the Prime Minister who, on October 17, last year, told DEMBA he would make them go to arbitration by passing legislation if they did not agree voluntarily.

It was the personal intervention of the Prime Minister, on behalf of the workers, that resulted in the Tyndall arbitration tribunal being established.

The Prime Minister kept his promise to the workers to have the Tyndall Award made. Now we read from the so-called "Voice of the Workers" objections to the retrenchment benefits contained in the award. Who do they really speak for? Where were they when the Prime Minister was fighting the cause of the workers last October against ALCAN? What sinister motives guide them to object now to retrenchment benefits, demanded by the workers over a year ago, now finally obtained?

If ever there has to be retrenchment, it will be the result of fear mongers deliberately causing confusion amongst us with the aim of reducing production to serve the interests of their foreign masters and mentors.

The Minister of Mines and Forests has announced the new company's management. Where are these "political appointees" complained of? Where is this "victimization" we are being warned of?

It is time for us to face the truth, ugly as it may be, that those who seek to spread fears and cause dissension now are those who now seek to sew the seeds of confusion for ALCAN to reap the benefits.

The People's National Congress says: Stand firm now. Let's get on with the job. Let's show the Prime Minister our metal.

Let's produce more and better bauxite NOW.

Let's turn our Alumina into Aluminum SOON.

Let's reap the benefits for ourselves and Guyana.

Workers Solidarity Committee
(GMWU Hall, Linden: 16 August, 1971)

Comrades and General Public,

At a meeting held on July 27th, 1971, workers and members of the GMWU decided by a unanimous voice to expel Misters Orrett, Gaskin, and Ashton Angel from the Ten Man Solidarity Committee, which was set up after the April strike to clean up our

Union of the evils of maladministration, etc.

This decision was taken after it was disclosed that Angel and Gaskin had acted in a manner which was harmful to the interest of the workers at Linden.

Acting on rumors to the effect that these two members had gone to the residence of the Prime Minister at Belfield House, the Committee summoned them to a meeting, because not only was this rumor in circulation, but workers were accusing the entire Committee of insincerity and dishonesty. Shortly after the visit to Belfield, these two workers spoke at a meeting at which Minister Jack was present. On the Monday following, a newsletter was circulated which caused a tremendous amount of criticism of the Committee by the workers.

Angel and Gaskin admitted receiving a phone call from the PM and going to Belfield House. In the midst of their hostility and arrogance, they said that they were at liberty to do whatever they wanted and would make no apologies for their actions. The Committee meeting agreed to bring this behavior of two members to the notice of all workers.

The Committee wishes to state that any member of that body can call a meeting to discuss any business affecting our present struggle, and therefore finds it extremely suspicious indeed when these two crept off to Belfield House and sneaked to Linden without its knowledge. The suspicions of the Committee are further deepened when out of the thousands of workers of Linden, these two were invited by the PM to Belfield.

Knowing that the Committee was appointed by the workers to look after matters directly related to the workers, why did Angel and Gaskin act in such a conniving manner? Was it not their duty to inform the workers of the PM's request and to guided by the workers' decision?

Angel and Gaskin have claimed that their visit to Belfield House was of a "private and personal" nature. Yet they admitted that they discussed with the PM matters affecting the "entire community." Angel in particular said that he "thought that was an opportunity to present our case to the PM." Gaskin, for his part, said that he made it "quite clear" to the PM that anything said during the discussions represented his "own views."

They should have known that had it not been for the existence of the Committee, Angel and Gaskin would just have been names of faceless persons. They have become "famous" solely because of the Committee which is actively involved in a struggle and not because of their "personal, private" lives.

True to their nature, these two rushed off to the press, claiming that they have resigned from the Committee and accused "certain elements" of "not acting in the best interests of good trade unionism" and of being "anti-government." The conduct of Angel and Gaskin can in no way be that of responsible workers who sit on a representative body. Their conduct, particularly from the Belfield incident onwards, leaves much to be desired, and moreover smacks of a selfish and opportunistic urge to hit the headlines. It is they who have not acted in the best interest of the workers who placed them on the Committee. As for the part of being "anti-government," it is very foolish for Angel and Gaskin to accuse anyone of being "anti-government," for unless their memories are very shallow, they will recall whenever workers—not only at Linden, but on the waterfront, sugar estates, Civil Service, Police Forces, or even Mrs. Dasent—stand up for the what is right and just, they are accused by those who seek to deny them their rights , of either "embarrassing the Prime Minister," "undermining the economy," or of being "anti-government."In the light of what is taking place in Guyana today, such accusations are commonplace and therefore have no meaning to the "The Wretched of the Earth."

The Committee states clearly and unapologetically that the workers on July 27th, 1971, REJECTED the offer by Ashton Angel and Orrett Gaskin to Resign and instead EXPELLED them from the Ten Man Solidarity Committee. The Committee fully endorses this decision and pledges to continue the struggle despite the obstacles, renegades, crooks and place-seekers, until victory is won.

Solidarity with all Workers.

Aston Angel and Orrett Gaskin
(16 August, 1971)

Fellow workers, misinformed comrades, we bring to your attention, for your information, for the benefit of our community and the future of this entity, the facts.

Anyone participating in activity which is an apparent design to agitate unnecessary industrial unrest in an effort to create economic unbalance and instability, consequently weakening the financial resources of the government with intention of overthrowing it, could be considered taking part in acts of treason. Any group of groups using workers general support to perpetrate a personal vendetta against any government should be scapegoated. Fellow workers, let us not support these selfish people with their political vendetta who would like to see the PNC government on its face. These opportunists are trying to create an inability of the government to run this entity, and are using our general support as their political weapon. Comrades, these people are not fighting the executives of the GMWU, for which you have vested them with the authority on your behalf; these people are fighting the government. If the workers are involved in an internal trade union dispute, they should sensibly see that it remains as such and not be extended for the benefit and satisfaction of a few. All patriotic minded workers ought to realize their role in the society and live up to their responsibilities.

Our honor is loyalty—loyalty to the workers' struggle when there is a justified cause for a fight. Our honor is loyalty—loyalty to the government of Guyana when the workers do not have a fight. Nothing can change this. Because of these circumstances, there developed very quickly, a "committee in a committee" situation. Behind what was apparently an iron front of a well organized functioning committee, there was a willed division. Whether the fostering of such a division was due to calculated cunning or a more generalized intellectual dishonesty is left to be ascertained.

We recall quite clearly Desmond Moffatt saying, in no uncertain terms, that he "breathes hate and would fight Burnham and his government eating grass." After a meeting held by the Minister of Mines and Forests to announce Vesting Day at the Mackenzie Primary School, we were grossly criticized by Moffatt and Goodluck because we pledged our firm support to nationalization on behalf of the workers. They were against the newsletter dated 12 July which supported nationalization. All Keith Goodluck speaks about is "Jagan said" and what "Jagan said." This has happened since his three-hour talk with Jagan negotiating strike relief during the strike. Morris Frank has subjected himself to being impressed by the aforementioned two and supports their ideas blindly and absolutely. Imagine, these people are against us speaking with the Prime Minister of this country. We hereby publicly denounce their ideals.

Moreover, what was frighteningly amazing is whichever part of the committee acted, this was truly accepted as being representative of ten persons. Consequently, there were very often conflicts and internal disputes. The Committee had become a regime. After an unwavering scrutiny of all these discoveries, our attitude was one of cold curiosity and extreme reserve. We decided to resign. This was our duty.

White Man Attempts Rape
(ASCRIA—Wismar Compound, Newsletter 7, Undated 1970)

We are particularly happy at the response of workers to a problem involving our Sisters at the Student Nurses Hostel.

In a comradely and cooperative manner, we have demonstrated our determination to protect Guyanese womanhood from the North American cannibals who infest our community.

We are all aware of the facts. On Saturday, July 18th 1970, a few of our Sisters discovered a white man in their sleeping quarters trying desperately to gain entry into the room occupied by two Sisters. They raised an alarm and the white culprit tried to evade apprehension by hiding in a toilet. He was caught however as he sought to escape through a window by removing louvers.

The time was 1:30 AM and the man was almost naked (he had on only a brief). He was handcuffed by a Town Council Constable and handed over to DEMBA's Security Officer, who upon learning that he was DEMBA staff promptly released him and assisted him to get his pants. Our Sisters naturally protested at the man's release and they were threatened by a DEMBA Security Sergeant with prosecution for disorderly behavior.

Later DEMBA's Medical Superintendent asserted that the man was probably invited by one of our Sisters. However, as the absurdity of his remark dawned upon him, he claimed that the man was a drunk and "strayed." To account for the man being naked, the company modified this excuse by claiming that he went for a swim (at 1:30 AM!).

This is not the first incident of this sort. About two weeks ago another white man invaded the hostel in bright daylight and, like a rooster chasing hens in the farm-yard, he had a dozen of our Sisters running "helter skelter" for the safety of their rooms.

In 1969, the hostel was invaded by a white bandit who waved a revolver at them, demanding a woman.

138

We know that management is responsible for the safety of our Sisters at the hostel and if they abrogate this responsibility then we are prepared to grant our Sisters adequate protection.

We wish to state quite clearly that in the future, if any white savage, in an attempt to satisfy their carnivorous intentions, happens to "stray" uninvited and unencouraged to the confines of the living quarters of our Sisters, we will make very certain that they never find their way out.

Dr. Roza's Attitude Toward the Students
(Undated, 1970)

Dr. Roza and Matron had agreed to represent the Student Nurses in all aspects of grievance.

In this he has failed.

When informed about the incident on July 18, 1970, Dr. Roza's reply was:

1) Did you know the man?

2) Contact the Administrator.

On the eighteenth, around 8:00 AM, two nurses were sent to Dr. Roza's office to speak on behalf of the Student Nurses. These nurses were Goodchild and George. They demanded deportation of the intruder.

The questions were:

1. "Are you sure the nurses did not invite the man?"

2. "Are you sure that none of the nurses were friendly with him?"

3. "Did he not knock on the wrong door?"

4. "Do you not believe that it's too dastric a measurement to deport the intruder?"

5. "Do you want an apology, or more than an apology?"

The representatives rejected the suggestion of apology. Dr.

Roza left for discussions with management. A few minutes later, we heard the telephone apology was accepted. Dr. Roza returned later and nothing was said concerning the matter.

Four hours elapsed, while we were still waiting for the results of the meeting.

Throughout the waiting period, eight to ten nurses slept in one room, owing to fear and apprehension due to lack of protection.

On Sunday night, we demanded security and protection from te Administrator. This concession was granted.

PREVIOUS INCIDENTS

1. In October 1968, a nurse was raped. When confronted about security measures, Dr. Roza said the nurses would soon get pregnant for the constables.

2. In May 1969, a white man entered the hostel with a revolver, demanding a woman. The nurse, confronted, hid in her wardrobe. No security was granted, in spite of more requests. No action was taken.

3. In July 1969, the nurses requested to be in a union, owing to some grievances. Dr. Roza's reply was: "Set it out of your heads, because you are students, you cannot have a union to represent you."

4. In December 1969, a man entered the hostel, tapped on a nurse's door, when the door was answered, he made no reply and he left. The matter was reported. Nothing was done.

5. In September 1969, a white man entered the ward, proclaiming to be Dr. Da Silva, a doctor. He arranged the charts, went tot he semi-private room and massaged a woman's abdomen. This exercise produced hemorrhage in the patient. She had just delivered.

The nurse on duty escaped into the female's dressing room. This matter was reported. No steps were taken. The nurse resigned.

6. In February 1970, a nurse was returning to work when a sailor saw her and attempted to scramble her. She then ran into the dining room, where he followed. The House Mother, maids and nurses around, viewing the situation, seek refuge into rooms. One nurse was hiding in the bathroom and had he known to open the door, the nurse might have been raped.

8. **Additional:** A nurse visited Dr. Roza, suffering from fever and a pain to the throat. Waiting for him to examine her throat, the nurse was told to prepare for a general examination.

He then asked, " Are you sure you are not pregnant?" The diagnosis was tonsillitis. This question was asked because he stated previously that the nurses are whores and prostitutes.

9. Dr. Roza does not believe the nurses are really ill, until they collapse.

10. Discrimination between white and colored. Staff men and their families have the privilege of seeing Dr. Roza at any time. Colored and ordinary people cannot.

Appendix
*Selected ASCRIA documents
and additional writings by Eusi Kwayana
(1972-1974)*

Eusi Kwayana's *The Bauxite Strike and the Old Politics'* (1972) status as a classic of Caribbean radical history and political thought is not predicated on projecting truths for all time. Rather, the book's intellectual legacies are based on its capacity to ask questions which captivated that generation and will move the minds of the future. Kwayana documented a turning point in the racial insecurity of multicultural Guyana, and in assessments of class struggle and colonial freedom in the African world. A historical moment where a significant change is in process is not easy to recognize and record. Distinguished by the self-mobilization of the bauxite workers of Linden, as much as his own self-criticism, that fragment of time was distinguished by hard fought lessons. In Chapter Seven of this book, Kwayana humbly includes a collection of leaflets which document a transformation, in the late 1960s and early 1970s, and which first show Pan African and class struggle sentiment on the ground in uneasy coexistence, or in conflict. To some, this may seem an odd way to end such a transformational book. The reader may come to question whether there was in fact a direct democratic breakthrough at all. While Kwayana's introduction and the body of the book both clarify that there was indeed such a rupture, the following appendix further amplifies its content and quality. *The Bauxite Strike*, within which are included many labor actions by these industrial workers, concludes with an incipient rejection of ordinary party politics and an awareness that national liberation and workers self-management in a people of color led multiracial nation may be synonymous.

This appendix of selected ASCRIA documents and extra Kwayana writings of 1972-1974 are not of episodic value. Here is the evidence of an extended archive of political thought which evolved to a direct democratic perspective that began to be debated across the African world, and transformed the self-governing content of the movement for Black autonomy. Included here are ASCRIA's statement on "The Negative Direction in Guyana" (1973) which sums up the rupture with Forbes Burnham's PNC, a year after the original publication of *The Bauxite Strike*. This text reveals ASCRIA's participation in the fight against corruption and the cooperative movement in Guyana. It also partially explains the growing tension in the Caribbean over the global movement for the Sixth Pan-African Congress in Julius Nyerere's Tanzania. The ascendancy of Burnham, and other Caribbean statesmen as patrons of the Congress, revealed a decline in the autonomy of the activist delegation from the region, led by Kwayana, which was ultimately banned from attending for its class struggle perspectives which threatened Black led nation-states.

"The Bauxite City and the New Canadians" (1974) and "Toiler's Unite!" (1974) update *The Bauxite Strike* with a more comprehensive approach to the political economy of the industry and the Black working class' increasing suppression by both Black union representatives and Black managers after the nationalization of the industry had been completed.

Especially crucial are the documents related to the direct democratic multicultural rebellion of landless sugar workers of 1973. This forging of class struggle with both Indo-Guyanese and Afro-Guyanese grew out of the struggle against corruption, where the new Black Bourgeoisie, among other crimes, restricted access to homestead plots for the marginal cane farmers and unemployed, while reserving huge amounts of land for speculative ventures or great estates for themselves. An alliance of the multinational corporation, Bookers, and Burnham's PNC government attempted in the name of public welfare to sell modest lots back to the descendants of slaves and indentured servants.

By popular committees and councils, Eusi Kwayana and ASCRIA facilitated a rebellion against what they termed "feudal capitalism" through providing guidelines for a squatters movement that overcame racial insecurity and which expected the sugar workers could arrive on their own authority and govern themselves. "No More Exploitation by Bookers," a letter by Kwayana to a government minister, and "Getting Back The People's Land," an essay by Kwayana revealing how appeals to the government going back to 1964 to resolve the land crisis have gone unheeded, are opening shots which warned that ordinary people will soon take matters into their own hands. "Guidelines" (1973) reveals the direct democratic self-managing politics placed forward by ASCRIA. "Sugar and Redemption" (1973) illustrates the political economy of feudal capitalism. "The Declaration of Bachelor's Adventure" (1973) is a radical statement on the Guyanese situation, in contrast to the pseudo-socialism of Burnham's PNC and the spectre that AS-CRIA appears to wish to overthrow the government. This speech is placed in the historical context of racial insecurity between Indians and Africans which is in the process of being left behind. "Resolutions Passed" (1973) from a rally of people's committees, among other things, highlights the demand for cost-free transfer of lands, the victimization of squatters by the police, and rejection of the government's intention to racially divide the people. It also insists on social legislation which would increase taxation on Bookers' sugar corporation's revenues from global trade and redresses the historical grievances of non-resident sugar plantation workers.

The final document, "People Force PNC to Pay for Sugar Lands," deconstructs Burnham's public address subsequent to the landless cane farmer rebellion, and reveals that ordinary people pushed Burnham, and Bookers, from behind. This writing brings closure to our extended consideration of Guyana in the early 1970s, as a struggle distinguished by popular self-management.

Transitional demands were made as a prelude to independent labor action. Despite being met with brutality and repression, these demands were implemented on the authority of the workers themselves.

Matthew Quest
2012

ASCRIA Statement
on the Negative Direction in Guyana
(April 1, 1973)

1. ASCRIA announces today, for the benefit of those in doubt that we have come to a definite break with the PNC. In our opinion the PNC has betrayed the wishes and the interests of African people, and is engaged in a vicious betrayal and exploitation of the manual workers, farmers, and brain workers, and all true revolutionary principles. Its foremost leaders are almost without exception corrupt and live a life of personal plunder of public resources. As soon as we discovered this we warned the Party leaders about it (November 1970). When we saw that plans to punish corruption were farcical we attacked the Government publicly (June 27, 1971). The Government and the PNC gave the old colonial answer to our farsighted and principled attacks: Victimization, dismissal, political terror, starvation of our active members, and have active plans for the "elimination" of those who conduct revolutionary struggle. "You cannot be in ASCRIA and be in the PNC" because "You cannot be an ASCRIAN and live."

2. At the 1964 elections we gave total support to the PNC and played a great part in mobilizing the election support at home for the PNC. We gave African people the understanding that the Burnham Government would ease their economic burdens and set an example of clean and unselfish government. Later on we assured Africans abroad that Guyana was a refuge of the oppressed, in which a system to satisfy the needs of the people was being built.

3. As the PNC leaders gained more power they became more unfeeling, more drunk with power, more arrogant, more callous, more and more corrupt and more tied to U.S. imperialism and the

Bookers Sugar complex.

4. This document seeks to point out as briefly as possible why we find it impossible to be allies of the PNC, to criticize ourselves, and explain to the *African* people, first of all, and to the public, our mistakes, and to explain our attitude to election politics. Many of the points we make here will be explained in bulletins at greater length. We do not believe that our actions should be a mystery and wish to let all the African people know where they stand with us.

OUR PRACTICAL WORK

Apart from giving assistance in the election campaign, we kept the African people organized and politically educated. It is from us that the PNC masses learned about the need for the objectives of an economic revolution. It is from us that they understood the meaning of *liberation* politics and the need for all out social revolution. We preached collectivism and *ujamaa*, what in Eastern Europe is called socialism. It is very important to make the point that all PNC activists who did not learn from ASCRIA know nothing at all about revolutionary politics. The PNC leadership never teaches the people the way to liberation or people's power. They preach and practice *Leader's Power*.

At mass rallies (1969) called jointly by ASCRIA and the progressive wing of the YSM we mobilized the public and prepared it for radical change. At one such rally the Prime Minister, guest speaker, challenged our members to go into the interior and build a road. He claimed that some people were only "talking" about revolution. To his astonishment the brothers volunteered and became the spearhead group of the new thrust in the interior. They finished the road (Tumatumari-Konowaruk) in record time. Because of ideological differences, because the PNC officials only understood leader worship, and were at heart highly colonized snobs, The ASCRIA pioneers, although successful, came back to Georgetown out of favor with the PNC leadership.

MARUDI

ASCRIA worked hard to inspire our young men and women to support the PNC's interior occupation program. Many black youths responded and decided to break away from the coast and start a new life. The most significant of these truly cooperative settlements was Marudi. The members of Marudi organized for over 6 months before going into the South Rupununi, fully aware of the risk of attack from foreign countries. Among them were Marxists, Pan Africanists and Ujamaa socialists. They saw themselves as people building a new society. After making a 36 mile road they were advised by the P.M. to leave the road and build an air strip which they completed. They erected buildings for their wives to join them. They planted several acres of tomatoes, carrots, and other food crops. They had a collectivist leadership, classes in political economy, science, Swahili. They worked along with Amerindians and were inviting them to join the co-op. They made careful plans of everything and discussed these plans fully. Among them were many skilled, pioneer minded people, bent on building a community without any exploitation or snobbery. We write about Marudi because it is about the one about which we know most. Suddenly in January, 1971, along with other interior cooperatives not so well organized, Marudi was closed down. In closing these Co-op communities the Government, through Dr. Reid put its big boots on the new society. *It violated the <u>most basic</u> cooperative principle, economic self-determination.* No explanation was given, but various PNC leaders gave these reasons: (1) The interior settlements were not viable (2) The danger from Venezuela and Suriname had passed. (3) The interior co-ops were ASCRIA guerila bases. (4) The P.M.'s published remarks "Don't be like those jokers who squandered millions of dollars in the interior." (August

1972).

No respect for people, high handed pushing around of people, take-it-or leave it; that is PNC rule. And the an most responsible for this defeat of the classless society has been awarded by himself the Order of Excellence of Guyana. The Marudi settlement also was tied up with the world wide black revolution against imperialism and capitalism. African American students spent periods there trying to expel from their minds the problem of the USA, practicing self-reliance, learning to love the land, and teaching the structure of U.S. racism and imperialism. The chairman of the Coop was Masimini the freedom fighter. Not one of these interior pioneers has been charged with any offense but vile slander from the PNC is their reward.

EXAMPLE

So far from encouraging people not to work, ASCRIA went to several districts holding unemployment seminars. At the end of these the residents were always ready to look after themselves and use their land, if any, or to demand facilities from Government to make agriculture possible. We worked so hard at these things that PNC society-seekers felt we wanted to "take over." Tensions developed. But although we called for sacrifices we set the example and refused to live a life of social plunder.

LABOR

In the DEMBA strike of April 1970 we advised the PNC leader to listen to the cries of workers and to get off his high horse. Instead the PNC used all the repressive machinery against the strikers; police, troops, tear-smoke, arrest, court, everything. The PNC policy exposed itself as "Socialism in words, but social politics in deeds." The labor movement is treated like a crowd of children who are angry because they are not fed but who are thrown sweets to keep them from boiling over. The leading part of it is bought out in a systematic way and then expected to operate against the workers to keep on good terms with the PNC Government.

CORRUPTION

Some of the things we discussed could have been political mistakes. But the fall in corruption is not a political mistake. It is a deliberate choice of a gang of men who are determined to get rich off public office. They have thus made themselves a class and must be attacked as a class. In terms of social biology they are parasites. In moral terms they are thieves, brazen thieves, snatching bread out of the mouths of the poor. Since November 1970 ASCRIA demanded a war against corruption. It also called for a Code of Conduct for Ministers and Parliamentarians. On January 4, 1971 the Prime Minister Burnham, B.A., L.L.B., S.C., Order of Excellence (in deception of the people) said he had a Code "in draft." He also authorized the Ombudsmen to look into charges of corruption. In September 1971 he declared his definite, deep-seated snobbery. He said on radio, "There is a lot of corruption at the lower levels." On October 22, 1971 ASCRIA made complaints of "malpractices amounting to corruption" against two Ministers of Government, one African and one Indian. Corruption is Corruption. We see corruption as theft by a person who is in authority to hide his theft. The PNC style now is that no leader is allowed to remain clean – all those who refuse to get involved are secretly accused and fall into the bad graces of the Powers. So the web of corruption is spreading. It is doing great harm to the soul of the people. It is such a crime because corruption can kill <u>any social system</u>. No revolutionary should take it coolly. Marx always said "Death to the Big Thieves!" In our case the thieves are dealing death to those leaders who do not toe the line. In our considered opinion the conduct of the PNC leaders is a disgrace to Black people and affects our dignity.

THE SYSTEM

Published evidence shows that the system in Guyana is propped up by the U.S. and West German Imperialisms. The system is one which can be very dangerous in a small job hungry community. It is a very personal despotism, in which the leader does not flinch from calling people and threatening them personally with starvation and "ringing of their neck." This man who was never victimized by the colonial rulers, who was despised by the British and loved by the U.S. State Department, who has enjoyed and exploited every privilege colonial society cannot see the vile nature of victimization.

Guyana is run by one man who talks for the people and acts for himself, who no longer bothers to deny his personal wealth. The system is not complete without the Opposition leader who has cleverly cooperated with Burnham's crimes for the past seven years, and who is active again because of forthcoming elections. Each bases his party in his race group and tries to buy over the other race for personal glory. This process creates tensions and will have no sensible outcome for the people.

There is no socialist construction in Guyana. There has been no political revolution. The pre-colonial mulatto elements are still in high favor. The people in power, Burnham, Ramphal, Green, have a spiritual home in Europe. They play with the historical culture of the masses, and patronize those who can best misrepresent and caricature it.

Guyana is governed by the P.M., the political aristocracy, and the managerial elite and a whole group of male and female political prostitutes. Together they crush the spirit of the people, bully the people into submission, support and promote only the meanest and most spineless, maintain an elite that can do no wrong, build up a wall of privilege that excludes any but themselves and bend the kneed to the god of corruption and plunder.

The Burnham Government having nationalized DEMBA more

in a fit of anger than as a result of policy continues to run it as a capitalist enterprise. Not only this but it is paying to the owners in compensation all that they desired and millions more than it said it would pay. From the start, and in every crisis, the "nationalized" company has been shored up big by U.S. imperialism. So profitable was the compensation to the owners, ALCAN, the Canadian and the U.S.A. have ever since continued economic aid to Guyana. Robert Hamer, chief of USAID, makes no secret of the fact that he is the country's godfather and that he regards Guyana as a model among the developing countries. The relatives below the political elite and the U.S., Canadian, and West German diplomats are more than diplomatic. It is quite clear that they are very social and freely showing a close identity of purpose. Guyana's subtle defense of the U.S.A. at the Panama Security Council meeting is kind of political service to U.S. imperialism which Guyana renders in return for U.S. economic and political support.

Now that, the Forbes Burnham Ideological Institute has been established and is teaching the ideology of Burnhamism, it is our duty to analyze Burnhamism as far as it has revealed itself. This is important because what is now called Burnhamism is a clever national and international tactic of treachery from within by penetration from outside. Burnhamism noting ASCRIA's interest in the Africa slave descendants of the Western Hemisphere pretended to share a similar interest. With this pretense it infiltrated the Black Power movement, the Pan African Liberation movement and through friendship with Tanzania and Zambia the world wide movement for socialism against imperialism. In its home territory, Burnhamism has done nothing to liberate the descendants of African slaves from their economic bondage, but is making them feudal type dependents on the political elite. He has unleashed a war of victimization, dismissal, boycott, surveillance against the many forces which tried to push the Guyana revolution to a position of egalitarianism and national and racial dignity, that is to say ASCRIA. He lured freedom fighters from Africa and Afro-America into Guyana to build his image as a model freedom fighter and is now expelling them just when the U.S.A. is less occupied in Vietnam, and can best deal and is dealing with Afro American revolutionary protest within the U.S.A. The Burnhamites do not on any issue put forward the advanced revolutionary line. And they are intolerant of this line and persecute those who advocate it, thus helping in forces of backwardness inside and outside the country. It is in this spirit that Burnham closed down Marudi Cooperative while maintaining the feudal cooperative directly under his control. It is in this spirit that the registration of a small Pan African cooperative press established in the U.S.A. was brazenly refused on the ground that Afro Americans and the South African brother were non-citizens. The chairman of the Marudi group was also one of the members of the press which also included Guyanese. In the spirit of suppressing the advanced revolutionary line acceptable to the people, it victimizes anyone who is known to be taking an active part in the fight against corruption denying them even appointments fitting their academic standing. In the height of a corruption hearing against a Minister, for example, the Government dismissed a key witness, a lorry driver, and replaced him only because the minister's lawyers explained that the clumsy act would embarrass them at the hearing.

WHAT, THEN, IS BURNHAMISM?

Burnhamism is disguised treachery, disguised class snobbery, and disguised feudal capitalism, infiltrating the ranks of revolutionary movements and trying to soften them and corrupt them from within. It is the political vehicle of a middle class bent on establishing itself as a bourgeoisie of a special kind, while maintaining control of the working masses and deceiving them with the slogans of equality, the "small man becoming a real man," "feeding, housing, and clothing the nation by 1976." What the slogans do not show is that at every step the political elite exacts tribute from individuals and from the public resources ad even from cooperatives which were to be the instrument of emancipation. Its only relation to the working class is that of a labor aristocracy whose function is to manipulate the labor movement to dance to the tune of the rulers. Burnhamism is sweet-voiced, slogan mongering treachery, individualistic platform boasting and image building in an age of mass democracy, the liberation of grassroots energies and people's power. It seeks to disguise the glaring class contradictions by the invention of the neutral concept of "the small man" who the social snobs promised to make "a real man."

Burnhamism as an ideological category is essentially non revolutionary, but uses the mass political movement and the power it offers to promote an elite which had roots among the people and intimidate and harass the people in great detail. It is precisely because Burnham by its conception and tactics has a principle (the need for controlling the mass movement) that the flirtation with radicalism, socialism, culture posturing and so on has come about. Burnhamism is from its history fully aware of the scorn of the world revolutionary forces. It has felt this scorn and lived with it from 1955 to 1971.

Burnhamism is its victimization, and threats of repression makes out that it is repressing a counter-revolutionary force, but the PNC is a damper on the revolutionary spirit of the Africans. The nationalization of DEMBA, a deal very pleasing to ALCAN was accomplished without any right wing campaign in the country. Burnhamism's griping about forces opposed to revolutionary change do not apply to the mass movements which the PNC is attacking.

ASCRIA's mistake was to lead the African people to believe that once the problem of African solidarity was solved a people's political line would be followed.   Again we, especially our leadership, trusted too much in the platform declarations of the elite and our leadership was slow to believe rumors of corruption among Ministers.   It did not exercise the vigilance necessary always, and especially dealing with opportunists.   ASCRIA therefore, unwilling to risk a "split" remained silent at the PNC's doings and accepted rather weak excuses for the failures of the government to develop a mass line, to inspire the people and given them the right to govern. Since the Council of Compounds of September 1971 these mistakes are being corrected. Finally we lament the absences of a radical Indian organization which has the courage to criticize the PPP leadership as we are doing the PNC leadership. Many Indians are very ready to take the PNC to pieces, but utter not a word of criticism of Indian political leadership and the Indian based party. This factor, more than anything else, will hinder the movement for real power and authority of the workers and farmers. All revolutionaries who think it unimportant are skimming over the most vital political factor for the building of any kind of liberated economy and liberated society.

The PPP falsely calls itself Marxist-Leninist. Such a party thrives on criticism and self-criticism. We have read what Marxist parties thousands of miles away have said about their own mistakes. The PPP does not criticize itself for wrong policies and mistakes. It came out of the whole of the violence of the 1960s without a word of self-criticism. All it does is to blame others. Such a party cannot be regarded as a serious liberation party.

Because we do serious ideological work, those who confuse the public have called us a political party. We are not a political party. The only political party we supported was the PNC up to June 1971. We now have **no connection** with any of the election parties in Guyana.

Coordinating Council, ASCRIA
30 Third Street, Alberttown, Georgetown, Republic of Guyana

The Bauxite City and the New 'Canadians'
(*ASCRIA Bulletin:* May, 1974)

The former Demerara Bauxite Company (DEMBA), belonging to ALCAN, was bought from ALCAN in 1971. The government's decision was made during negotiations with ALCAN in Georgetown.

Many of us were so happy that we thought that socialism was near at hand.

Three years have gone by.

Conditions at the Bauxite Town are a disgrace to the Guyanese people. It is wrong to compare conditions now with what they were under the white man. The white exploiter has no right to rule us. His rule is out of the question. The question is: How are things shaping under the black rule? What kind of life is being created? Are we making a better life or a better man? Or, are we making a big pig pen, and running a rat race?

On February 23, 1974, the PM declared, "In nationalizing DEMBA, I place the fate of the country in the hands of the people."

These words came from his lips. They were a big lie. Instead of placing the fate of the country in the hands of the people, the government rushed to Rockefeller's Chase Manhattan Bank. This US bank came to the government's assistance with a $9 million loan soon after nationalization.

The deal has not yet been explained to the Guyanese people. All we know is that the loan helped to keep the nationalized bauxite firm going. It helped to keep the industry in the imperialist camp.

GUYBAU is part and parcel of the imperialist economy. Only a month or so ago, parliament approved a government guarantee of further USA loans of some $20 million to keep the nationalized bauxite firm going. Statistics show a general fall in production.

CLASS PREJUDICE

The ASCRIA classes which were at Wismar came to an end some time ago. But there are "Classes" at GUYBAU, the "socialist" city—social "classes" based on position, money and attitude.

In both 1971 and 1972, government statistics show a drop in employment of bauxite "operatives" over the first, second and third quarters. The year 1972, to the first quarter of 1973, showed a drop in the numbers of persons employed by the plant. Meantime, every report says that new class positions, hateful to the people, are taking shape. The Guyanese managers have a bad name. Positive managers are there but they are few, like a drop in the ocean. People understood the white discrimination and fought against it. The workers resent the attitude of the new managers. They call them arrogant. Much money has been wasted because many of the new managers, with their welcomed book knowledge, failed to increase knowledge by *learning from the people on the job.* There developed a kind of managerial terror. The workers continually complain of the lack of respect of the new managing group for anyone without academic papers. Sharp divisions developed in social life. Things reached the point of absurdity.

A notice from above, inviting enrollment into the famous snob school, said plainly that the children of workers below a certain rank would not be admitted. And all of this took place *after* nationalization. Rumors of the bringing in of white expatriates began to fill the air. In fact, it seems that three such persons were actually recruited. On the other hand, to be fair, it is said that the new "Black Canadians" (the new managing set) complain of Party terror, which upsets them a lot, and forces them to harass the people. While PNC groups are white-marketing[1] cooking oil all

---

1   A play on words referring to informal, or illegal, economy often called the "black market", meant to undermine the association of negativity with "black." -ed.

over the country, the GUYBAU farm is selling certain goods only to the "upper strata" of employees!

DECAY ALL AROUND

Apart from these individuals who have the strength to keep out of the rat race, the social circles are taken up in a grave situation. Vice, always a special problem, has shot up to new heights. No one at the top discusses any type of socialist morality. In fact, who can do it? The example of party leadership in Georgetown is followed to the letter, so far as corruption goes. At the local government level, reports of mismanagement of funds in the recent posts have began to circulate and increase. The police are investigating as big boys are not involved.

MORALE GONE

Morale has gone to the dogs. The courteous know that it is their duty to work. They are showing that. But, in every example of 25 persons, 24.5 seem to be saying that they have no joy in their work. There is a reign of fear. Terror and the victimization of the political dissidents is the order of the day. The massive labor force has lost morale to contribute to the party to buy *New Nation*, to show the flag, all of this has driven people underground. Everyone knows that there are spies around to report to the PNC any word on complaint. The people stay way from events. May Day, 1974, was boycotted by the whole community. The "large" attendance reported was made up of school children! The same response was seen in Georgetown, where the PNC leader was heckled from beginning to end.

The PNC is not strong. It is well financed and well armed. Everyone knows which minister directs the Guyana version of Grenada's Mongoose Squad. Everyone knows that several crates of arms have been stolen from the regular army and taken over by the irregular army of the PNC.

WORKING AND LIVING CONDITIONS

The cost of living in Guyana officially went up 13 percent in 1972 and again in 1973. The rampant white market adds at least 12 percent for each year. In Guyana, food imports are banned before the new crop begins to grow. People are told—correctly—about colonial tastes. But everyone knows that the political elite can import apples, sardines, corned beef and have stores of these things (these are not personal attacks, but a description of the system, the greed, selfishness and the slave master's attitude). Food shortages are the order of the day. The ministers say there is no food shortage, but how can they know when their pantries and store-rooms are full? Government statistics show that between 1971 and 1972 the price of steak moved up 46 points, cassava 68 points, eddoes 9 points, onions 43 points, plantains 40 points and yams 36 points. When the national average is 40 points, the Linden figure is close to 65 points. But the Guyana Mine Workers Union, after a year of negotiations, could only "win" for the workers of the bauxite town a 5.6 percent increase in wages. Yet the ministers, after the 1973 election, pocketed increases of over 100 percent!

GUYANA'S RULERS

The people were exploited slaves under the Canadians, and now the black oppressors of the nation are Afro-Indian elites with "white" hearts and hopes under their shirt-jacks and dashikis. Whiteness is not a matter of skin color. It is a desire to enslave others.

The union of Afro-Indian oppressors, which rules Guyana under African corrupt leadership, does not want to see any unity among the African and Indian oppressed masses. *They will do anything to prevent it.* The boycott of May Day, and the heckling of the Prime Minister on May Day, show how the wind is blowing.

The workers at Linden must be true to their class. They

must not support this African Aristocracy and its allies of Indian businessmen. The salvation of the PNC is a lie. This lie pressures heavily on the thirty percent unemployed in towns, interior villages, and sugar estates. But it also pressures heavily on the bauxite area—correctly it now seems, named after the Prime Minister.

Workers must begin to search for an alternative!

TOILERS UNITE!
(*ASCRIA Linden Special:* Vesting Day, July 14, 1974)

"But I think it is also true that our successes since Vesting Day led in 1973 to the development of a certain level of complacency among our employees, which played its part, along with adverse external factors, in producing the indifferent, overall results of 1973. We have instituted and begun to implement a program to counter this feeling of complacency…"

Mr. Pat Thompson,
Chairman of GUYBAU
1973 Annual Report and Accounts

BOOK MANAGERS

On February 23 1971, the Prime Minister declared, "In na-tionalizing DEMBA, I place the fate of the country in the hands of the people." But according to Thompson, "early success" led to "a certain level of complacency among our employees." What about the sky high prices of consumer goods in Linden? What about the lack of ordinary water? Is it complacency Mr. Thompson? "Com-placency" means "quiet satisfaction; smugness." Let us see what the workers at nationalized Guyana Bauxite Company have to be "complacent" or "quietly satisfied" about. Of course they have their Chairman. They have the whole management team of other super-salaried New Canadians, who understand only management by terror. The book managers are too proud to learn from the foremen who long experience on the job. A letter from a GUY-BAU worker, published in ASCRIA Bulletin, says that the worker has less job satisfaction now than before the purchase of the company from ALCAN. This is disappointing. The place is swarming with agents who report to their chiefs any remark which is out of line. The PNC regards the industry as belonging not to the country but to the PNC.

UNION LEADERSHIP

The Union leadership has long sold out to the government. To secure itself, it has killed union democracy so that the President is not again to be selected by the general membership. Twice in the last six weeks workers used the strike weapon to get justice against the high handed actions of the management. It is an open secret that before negotiations begin, the union leadership (President and Secretary) are called in by the "Kabaka" (as the Prime Minister calls himself) and told to "hold the line" as there is no money. As a result, the Union accepted increases from the management of a mere 5.2 percent. Then 5% surtax is taken out, that increases the amount to .2 percent. This is supremely capitalistic exploitation. These things lead not to "complacency" but perhaps to frustration. But is easy to blame "our employees." Failure of management always discourages workers. A clue to the overall failure in the planning at Cabinet level can be seen from the report of the Treasurer Mr. Aravamudha Krishnan. He says, "a highlight of this year's performance is the spending of $14.71 million on capital account from internal resources of the company in pursuance of a program of replacing and modernizing equipment…" —equipment bought from ALCAN for some millions above the written down book value in a so-called nationalization. It is clear to everyone that the government has greatly overpaid for a lot of junk. (An even worse situation will soon come to light in Guyana Timbers—bought from the Commonwealth Development Corporation and now in need of complete re-equipment.)

Guyana is teaching a very anti-revolutionary lesson to the Third World. In the developing countries, many admire Guyana because the country boasts of building "socialism" with US support. PNC leadership has capitalized on being regarded by the USA as the means of keeping PPP and "communism" out of power. Now the USA is rethinking this policy. While Guyana's Foreign Minister and Prime Minister prattle a lot of liberal ideas and pass them off as socialism, they are busy tying Guyana up in the web of imperialist finance. GUYBAU has close financial relations with the US Export-Import Bank, Chase Manhattan and also Royal Bank Trust Company. Soon after "nationalization," Chase Manhattan Bank came to the rescue of Guyana's mock socialists. The excuse of PNC is that Chase, Coca-Cola and US finance are now entering the USSR and Eastern Europe. This is the business of the countries concerned—up to a point. Those who oppose it are called "Left opportunists." Yet, one must be quite insane to think that imperialist penetration in a Caribbean country will not do far greater damage than it can do in the massive USSR. Yet the "socialist" neo-colonials think that our weak economies can stand as much poison as the very strong Soviet economy. When the USSR allows US economic imperialism to penetrate the Soviet economy, it is of course, helping to make world imperialism stronger and harder to defeat. It is also giving neo-colonial governments a ready excuse for inviting imperialist penetration. It is very comical to hear countries like Guyana crow and compare themselves with a country like the USSR We have not yet defeated imperialism. That is the big difference. For all its revision, the USSR first made a clear break with imperialism, transformed its economy and is now taking chances.

PRODUCTION 1971-1973

Between 1971 and 1973, the output of metal grade bauxite, calcined bauxite and calcium alumina fell. In the light of this overall fall in production, Chairman Thompson's target is "to ensure the return in 1974 to the levels of productivity and profitability which we achieved in 1972." Thompson avoids setting 1971 as a target because of the "complacency" of the employees. But he never gives another important reason. The industry's hopes are based on "the Western world" that is, on world imperialism. Thompson says that GUYBAU's "recovery depends on fuel costs and also on whether fuel costs "will trigger an economic recession in North America and Western Europe." Thompson adds: "If the Western World does not for one reason or another slip into recession—thereby constraining a good deal of our output—or spiral into runaway inflation—thereby sending the costs of imported machinery and other inputs inordinately high—then I think GUYBAU stands a good chance..." There you have it. If Imperialism sneezes, GUYBAU will catch cold. Their blood stream is one and the same bloodstream.

BOOK VALUE

To justify the high price paid for DEMBA, a great deal of "bookwork" is going on with the valuation of assets. Experts in this area can render a service by inspection of the accounts.

EXPENSES

What explanation is there for the increase in "Administrative, selling and General Expenses" from $2.8 million in 1972 to $4.6 million in 1973 for a lower level of output? Surely this is not a result of the fuel crisis – the new Satan of our times. Again, "cost of sales" rose in 1972 by about 12% while profits fell by about 31%. How can this be explained when gross revenue rose by nearly $7 million?

THE WORKERS

Mr. Hubert Jack, technocrat Minister responsible to the Prime Minister only, tries to cover up the extremely capitalistic tendency of the report. He writes a message to keep the socialist "image" bright. He mentions "criticism and self-criticism" to appeal to the Eastern Europeans and "workers' participation" to appeal to the clever West German capitalists. He says "nationalization is not socialism" but "it is a step to socialism." Then he promises what the workers have already: "ultimately… they will be fully involved in the various aspects of the Company's activities." They act. They are involved in activities. But they do not control. Of course this is a lot of hypocrisy and an attempt to keep militants quiet. Why has the PNC not tried out workers' control at the various State Corporations, many of which existed before independence? They have not tried out any serious worker participation. This weekend the government announced a plan for workers to elect a representative to corporation boards instead of a hand-picked union representative. This does not mean workers control or participation. Other things have to be done first.

When we look at it deeply, we see that you cannot build socialism in one industry, although you can in one country. The Sugar Industry has not changed since 1763, in spite of 9 years of independence and 4 years of the Cooperative Republic. Although the sugar workers are more oppressed with low wages, the rate of profit extraction at GUYBAU exceeds the rate in sugar. One of the obstacles in the way of the bauxite workers is the imperialist ownership, not only of Reynolds, but of the sugar plantations. We cannot build socialism piecemeal, because capitalism does not stand still. GUYBAU workers suffer extreme class discrimination at the hands of the New Canadians. Sugar workers suffer extreme oppression under the New Scotsmen, who run more and more plantations. To begin with, the GUYBAU workers must give active support to the fight of GAWU for recognition in the sugar industry. Unity among the people who labor in these two industries for a start, is the foundation of people's power.

SATISFIED WITH THE USA

In a July 4th message to President Nixon of the USA, Prime Minister Burnham said, "May I take this opportunity to express my satisfaction with the spirit of friendship and cooperation that has characterized our relations at the bilateral, regional, and international levels."

No More Exploitation by Bookers
(*ASCRIA Bulletin*: December 5, 1972)

The following letter has been sent by ASCRIA to the Minister of Local Government on the question of an age-old system of robbery:

Honorable A. Salim,
Minister of Local Government,
Georgetown

Dear Minister,

It seems that your government is entirely without an understanding of the old villages and their land problems. All plans to buy land from the sugar plantations should be stopped. It is a pre-nationalization policy and we can take it no more.

The alliance between the government and the foreign sugar companies is a colonial-type alliance, which allows the foreign sugar companies to fleece the people by selling back to us our own lands, already bought by 250 years of slave labor.

Land required by the coastal villages for their expansion must be taken from the sugar producers by government free of charge and at no cost. There must be physical safeguards against squatting and the lands must be transferred in an orderly way, free of cost to the district councils, village communities, or cooperative societies, as in the case of Buxton and Haslington. Shall we, who struck the lion of ALCAN down, pay homage to the wolf of Bookers?

Secondly, it is an important principle of our revolution that the Sugar Industry Labor Welfare Fund must develop housing areas on behalf of "labor workers" (cane farmers and sugar workers) living in the villages. Any going back on this is a naked betrayal of our rights.

Villages, like Bachelor's Adventure, from which land was stolen in the past, must be given back all their lands as far as the Lamaha Canal. Villages, like Stewartville and Den Amstel, must be given lands for expansion.

The PNC cannot run out its second term of office and leave the Sugar Barons in control. Give us back our land.

Eusi Kwayana
Coordinating Elder, ASCRIA

Understand clearly that we support the developing of land for resident sugar workers, at no expense to them. But the same must be done for non-resident sugar workers. The resident sugar workers are mainly Indian. The non-resident are mainly African. But, we are attacking the system by which the sugar plantation still controls land, as it did one hundred years ago. The plantation belongs to the people!

Guidelines:
To Those Who "Discover" (or Seize) Sugar Lands
(1973)

1. The land to be seized is sugar land. Make some attempt to find out if the land you need is sugar company land.

2. If you find out for certain that you are not on sugar lands, but on privately owned land, leave it at once.

3. If they say that the land you took was given to a co-op, get the co-op members to come and negotiate with you on the basis for no payment for the land.

4. Watch the Official Gazette to see if titles are being passed suddenly over your head.

5. This is a people's movement. You cannot leave out people because of their party membership. But, if they are undermining the move, do not put them on the committee. This is not a movement against the government or the opposition, but against feudalism—sugar as landlord.

6. Each area must appoint a People's Committee. This committee must be allowed to meet and discuss matters by itself.

7. This committee must report fully to all the people. If things are going well, tell the people. If things are going badly, tell the people.

8. There must be strict rules about who can take up land. The landless people must be served first. There is no reason for speculators. If you have land, you cannot come before a comrade who has none. The committee must limit the number from each house.

9. Each group, after taking over an area, must measure it. Then, leave out place for streets and reserves. Then you can

decide on the size per lot. The lots must be equal in size. This is an equality movement.

10. You have created history. You are not in a new party. You are in an important movement. Feudal capitalism must go. You must destroy it and a piece of land and more strength will be yours. If they jail you or persecute you, they are making you a hero of your people. Your people need heroes. ASCRIA is not seeking your membership or your vote.

11. There will be communities dominated by Indians. The will be communities dominated by Africans. Whoever is the majority must protect the minority.

12. Where the same land is required by an African and an Indian community, we must first make an equal division of the sugar lands. There can be no agreement without equality.

13. You should aim at a homestead garden later on.

14. The various communities will come together to form the Free Land Council.

15. Begin to fence and build as soon as the committee has lotted out the place.

16. ASCRIANs are strongly cooperative people. To form a co-op now will not work. If the do not like your face, your co-op will never be registered. This can be proved.

17. Bookers has stated that it has handed lands over to the government free of cost for agriculture, housing and education (Guyana Graphic, January 20, 1973,1) government says that your action in discovering the land has shown them your need for land (New Nation, January 20, 1973). Keep it up.

18. ASCRIA's demand has therefore been accepted in principle—land free of cost. What is all the fuss about?

19. Important: Government forms can be filled out by those who are on the land. But, you must say you are paying nothing for the land. Write at No. 10, clearly: "No money for land. No deposit on land."

Getting Back The People's Land
by Eusi Kwayana
(*Guyana Graphic:* Sunday, February 25, 1973)

On January 22, 1973, the Deputy Prime Minister Dr. Reid, broadcast to the nation. His broadcast was aimed mainly at the squatters, who had taken over 250 acres of land. They had responded to ASCRIA's call for revolt against feudal capitalism and for the taking of sugar lands "without money, without price, and at no cost." Dr. Reid described the effects of the action in this way: "Organized attempts are now being made to create confusion and disturbance calculated to lead to the breakdown of the present state of tranquility."

The land seizure has been very orderly. The squatters acted more or less within the terms of "guidelines" put out by an organization. People travelling along the East Coast public road saw only Indian squatters. Why? They were an overspill from overcrowded Indian settlements or new villages along the public road. There were also African squatters along the public road from Lilliendaal, and Indian squatters at Plantation Ogle far south of the railway line. The areas of heavy African squatting—Vryheid's Lust, La Bonne Intention, Annandale, Vigilance—could not be seen from the public road.

The remarkable thing about the squatting was that squatters Indian and African followed ASCRIA's guidelines wherever competition between them seemed likely. The best lands to be discovered were to the south of the railway line at Annandale, La Bonne Intention and Lusignan. In the first two cases those areas were divided by the Peoples Committees equally between the two communities.

It is here that the "right wing" came into view, but these were well outside the ranks of the squatters. The African "right" felt that it was foolish to invite the Indians to divide the land equally. The

Indian "right" felt it was foolish of the Indian to agree because the lands were on the plantation and by "right" Indian property. They might even have said "for sugar workers only." This is the spirit which supports foreign exploitation all over the world.

Except for a few isolated cases, speculators, were absent from the movement. Most of the few speculators were to be found in the Vryheid's Lust area. They were not hard to find. They all were willing to pay for the land. Only a very few among all the squatters, apart from the speculators, were willing to pay for the land.

In terms of racial distribution it is possible that Africans claimed about 101 acres and Indians about 139 acres before the government intervened, as it claimed, to maintain tranquility.

As we see, there was no breach of tranquility at all. People on the East Coast and especially the squatters were very puzzled to find out where the "present state of tranquility" had broken down, or was threatened to break down. As for clashes between the squatters, the police say they had received no such reports. Where had the government and Dr. Reid received such information? Does it not remind you of the reasons given by the British and Bookers in 1953 for the suspension of the Constitution?

Not until the Chairman of Bookers spoke at Corriverton on February 19 was it made clear what tranquility the landless movement threatened to breakdown. A radio station was keen enough to report to Mr. Ellis, Chairman of Bookers in Guyana as saying: "We have no problem with the government of Guyana." The chairman also said that the relationship between the company and the government was different from the usual relationship in Third World countries. When the Prime Minister spoke he said that "the cooperation from Bookers has been heartening."

It is now clear that the tranquility which the squatters were likely to upset was the tranquility between the government and Bookers. Bookers is very wise to maintain peace with a government which allows it to maintain feudal practices. The fact that the unused lands cannot be a big issue with sugar, raises the most disturbing suspicions of what really is going on.

Why are the relations of tranquility between Bookers and the government hidden with such care from the public? In its attempt to convince the Guyanese people, Bookers declared that it had handed over to government free of cost, lands for housing, agriculture, and education. When the New Nation appeared, it admitted that lands had been handed over for those purposes, but it did not say "free of cost." Was the company telling such a brazen lie? Or was the New Nation lying by silence and omission? Where in Guyana has sugar land been handed over to the government for housing, free of cost? How had the government disposed of this land? Free of cost, or at a price? And if Bookers is lying, why does not the government expose Bookers?

It is merely so as not to upset the "tranquility" that reigns between the government and Bookers? Why are all these facts not know to the people? Why have the people to pay for developing land where they gave free labor to help develop it? Have the principles and objectives of self help been revised also? Why are all those things hidden from the people who are affected by them? Why is anyone in a committee who questions these things told that he is going against the Prime Minister? Is it slavery again?

I was personally in touch in 1964, with sugar workers who found it necessary to remove from Enmore and South Haslington. As Africans were afraid to squat in those days they approached the estate management as sugar workers, and resident sugar workers at that. They were given no assurances. That was in 1964. The Africans who squatted at South Haslington were sugar workers who had to give up Sugar Industry Labor Welfare lots and got to other estate land already laid out.

In spite of (or because of) the orderly discussions between SPA and the government the people of South Haslington to this day have not been given lots by the Industry or the Fund – after eight years. Some of them have recently been told that they must buy the new lots. Whoever raises these questions is accused of splitting the Africans, and wanting to become Prime Minister.

The political system gives no answers, discusses nothing, explain nothing to the people does not permit serious questions. When officials are asked to account to the people for their actions are called disloyal, ASCRIAN, enemies of the Prime Minister, anti-government or threatened with a beating, even by such dignified people as male district chairmen and finance officers. So after eight years in spite of orderly discussions in peace and tranquility between Bookers and government a simple problem like that of South Haslington has not been settled. Must anything more be said to justify the land campaign?

The SPA in reply to ASCRIA's letter invited the organization to address the demand for Sugar Industry Welfare benefits for non-resident sugar workers and cane farmers to the Sugar Industry Welfare Fund Committee.

I have among my papers, a letter dated 17th July, 1964 forwarding to the Secretary, Sugar Industry Labor Welfare Fund, Georgetown the following resolution: "Whereas sugar workers and cane farmers resident at Buxton-Friendship do not enjoy the benefits open to the workers resident on the sugar estate: Be it resolved that the cane farmers of Buxton-Friendship request the Sugar Industry Labor Welfare Fund and Enmore Estate Ltd., to develop the area East of Buxton-Friendship as a housing scheme for sugar workers and cane farmers resident in Buxton-Friendship." Mover: Councillor P. Hosannah; Seconder: J. Roberts (cane cutter). The meeting was held at then County High School, Buxton. A similar letter was sent to the SPA and to the Administrative Manager, Enmore Estate Ltd., signed by Sydney King.

Similar resolutions were moved in other villages. Some years after, the village councils themselves moved resolutions attacking the relationship between labor workers and the plantation.

In the meantime, applications for house lots by young people on the sugar plantation have been piling up, and this is now a living issue on the plantations.

At the same time, every plantation is moving its cane fields nearer to the people's homes, much to the resentment of the people. The villages are in a similar situation. People are being taxed out of reason. Land is scarce and very expensive. Unemployment rivals that on the plantation.

If the Indian workers and farmers were to be made comfortable and the African workers and farmers were to be neglected, there could be no kind of peace. If the African workers and farmers were to be comfortable and the Indians were to be neglected, there could be no kind of peace. The land campaign taught the country how to use imperialist property to solve racial contradictions which were in the first place created by the development of many imperialist properties.

A revolutionary government would have not thought first about its "image" or about supposed secrets leaking out, or about a plan to overthrow the government but would have seen the revolutionary potential of the action and supported it. Here was a chance for the people's army to show its revolutionary mettle by moving in to help the peasants secure the land and to extend the movement.

But no, the police were sent in against the people and the People's Army was said to be standing by to stamp out the peasants' revolt against feudal capitalism. It would have seen the revolutionary possibilities of using imperialist property for solving the contradictions between Africans and Indians. The Government's action against squatters amounted to a confidence trick.

"Government is taking possession of all sugar estates lands which are not beneficially utilized," declared the Minister of National Development. The tranquility had been disturbed. It was in effect saying: "All right, Bookers, you stand aside from this. Let us deal with them. It is our land. If we throw them off now, they will say we are capitalist stooges. So we are taking over the land in order to deal with them in our own right. You need not fear. You will lose nothing…"

This is confirmed by Booker Chairman Ellis's statement, "Bookers had no problem with the Guyanese government," and also the Prime Minister's echo, "the cooperation from Bookers has been heartening."

One of the government's strong attacks on ASCRIA was on the demand that the land should be given to the people without cost. As Minister Steve Naraine said on January 24, 1973, the government was prepared to pay Bookers for the land, and in November-December, the government actually announced that it was buying the land from the sugar companies. It was this announcement that sparked ASCRIA's campaign of "not a cent for the sugar companies."

The government knows that it has opened its revolutionary intentions to question. It will now have to make a big gesture which can catch the world headlines. This gesture will have to be in regard to Sugar. We can expect a magnificent piece of bluff.

The opposition PPP, which should have made the no compensation issue a national issue, is busy doing detective work to stop the alleged proxy campaign. Meanwhile, the PNC will work things out with Sugar and present the country with a closed deal; not for discussion. What the PNC-style revolution is doing for people is becoming clearer from daily experience.

The people of North Haslington, a PNC-strong hold, voted at a meeting to reject the free-land campaign because it would offend the Prime Minister if they supported it. So the PNC is using its supporters' loyalty to help the rich get richer and the poor get poorer. What matters is the people's loyalty to the party, not the party's loyalty to the people.

The leaders must be able to tell the bourgeoisie (the exploiters): "They are loyal to our party. We can get them to pay for the land. Do not worry with those self-seeking and irresponsible people who want to rob you sugar people of your just price. We have not been elected by the people to betray our pledges to you sugar people. You can sleep in peace and tranquility. Your co-operation has been most heartening…" And the Sugar men reply: "We have no problem with the government of Guyana."

Sugar and Redemption
(*ASCRIA Redemption Day Special:* February 17-19, 1973)

Economic revolution is not a slogan. It means overturning, shaking up, changing the economic system and the laws of the rich so that the poor people can be liberated, so that the poor can get relief from oppression.

Socialism means the production for usefulness rather than production for profits. It means the reason for doing things is to satisfy the needs of the people and not draw the people's blood to make fortunes.

When governments begin to talk about economic revolution and socialism the people have a right to demand and take certain things. If we cannot get one house lot from the Slave Plantation free of cost, the economic revolution is a fraud. We are not asking for freeness but for freedom.

During immigration, a few thousand Indians received free lands from the colonial government in place of return passage. Still today there are thousands of landless Indians. What about Africans who have never received any land free, never received compensation? Today, in the interests of good race relations and socialist unity based on equality we say: "Landless Africans and Landless Indians Unite Against Feudal Capitalism." Our meaning is as plain as the pasture. Our cry is as clear as thunder. Our tears are as rich as rain.

We do not respect any law which gives Sugar 200,000 acres of land. Is this a law of the revolution? No! It is colonial law. The same votes that voted that voted for the taking over of DEMBA are there to change that law. The PPP's support which was accepted for Bauxite must be accepted for Sugar. There is the power in the national assembly to take the land from Bookers, the main Feudal Capitalist.

What is feudal capitalism? The government has not tried to explain it. They told you Jimmy Cock Mek Ram Goat. That was their answer. Let us tell you about Feudal Capitalism.

Feudalism is a system of land holding. The King owns all the land. When you want land to work, you beg him and he gives you land. But you have to give him free labor several days a week. You have to use his factory. You have to use his court. You are bound to this kind just because he gave you a piece of land to work.

Capitalism is a system. It developed during Feudalism. It was supposed to crush feudalism and kill it. Capitalism is ownership of mines, farms, and factories by the rich who exploit the labor of workers, farm-laborers and miners, to make fortunes for themselves.

Bookers is *all two*. Sugar controls two hundred thousand acres of the best land on the coast. They cultivate one hundred thousand. They are the landlords of the Coast. Some of this land they stole from villagers, behind the backs of the people, like at Bachelor's Adventure. They dominate the land. They flood out their neighbors. They pour down poison from the air and ask you not to object to this. Bookers is capitalist also. They exploit labor. They store up reserves kept back by fraud (St. James) from the laborer and cane farmer. They have fields, factories, shops, everything except funeral parlors. So ASCRIA calls the system "feudal capitalism." They make feudal profits (from land) and capitalist profits (from business).

On February 11th Bookers opened its mouth. It said in the last 20 years Bookers developed 56,000 acres of land for cultivation. They said, "this represents a huge farming achievement for the nation." Which nation? They say that they "allocated" 2,550 acres to the Sugar Industry Welfare Fund. What is 2000 acres when Sugar cultivates 100,000 acres? They say 40,000 acres have been "released in recent years for beneficial occupation by the Guyanese people." *Yes and the Guyanese people are now groaning under this feudal capitalist burden.* Bookers talks to us scornfully of 25 acres given for this and 10 acres given for that. On February 11th Bookers opened its mouth. It spoke. But it said nothing...

"Every valley shall be exalted and every mountain and hill shall be brought low." (Isaiah 40:4) – That is revolution.

"He hath put down the mighty from their seat and hath exalted the humble and meek." (Luke 1:52-53) – This is revolution.

ALL THE LAND

We are not talking about unoccupied land. We are not talking about Bookers lef-lef and Bookers half mout. We are talking about the land God gave Guyana. We demand a revolutionary policy for all the land Bookers is squatting on. But there is quite a lot Bookers did not say. This poor company Booker McConnell Ltd. Had in December 1970 has reserves of $35 million (G). It is a big world company. In 1970 it had overdrafts of $40 million. Only $3.5 million was covered by security. This Company had fixed assets (solid property) worth $171 million. An Iten Freehold Land and Buildings is valued at $89 million, but their machinery and plant is valued at only $66 million. Their report has a note saying "Certain land overseas which under English law would be neither freehold nor leasehold has a balance sheet value of $17 million and is included in the $89 million." Bookers biggest involvement is in the Caribbean and that is mainly in Bookers Guyana.

In their mother country and Headquarters, England, Bookers has $117 million invested. In the Caribbean their investments amount to $150 million out of $189 million overseas. They are in U.K., Malawi, Nigeria, Zambia, Guyana, Jamaica, Trinidad, Canada and Brazil. But their biggest area/investment is in the heart of the Caribbean and their biggest profit is in the Caribbean. They made $4.8 million in the Caribbean out of $6 million made overseas. Profits made in Britain (UK) amounted to $3.3 million. This is Bookers, which they say cannot afford to hand over the land without payment. Remember, their reserves were $25 million at the end of 1970. Profits from sugar in 1970 amounted to $3.4 million and in 1969 sugar profits were over $4 million. In shops and light industries the same year, 1970, Bookers made $4.3 million in profits and $1.4 million in getting people drunk. The amount of money employed by Bookers in their business and trading assets increased from $32.9 million in 1961 to $61 million in 1970.

In 1970 Bookers held Guyana government securities worth nearly $65 million, that is money lent the government of Guyana. Between 1960 and 1966, sugar produced half the wealth in Guyana's annual production but paid only 7.4% of government revenue. (Clive Thomas). Thomas also says that there is more and more exploitation in Sugar. It is rapidly expanding acreage and production. It pays big dividends. It uses less and less labor. It pays less and less taxes. Its rate of investment is too small for its size…

These are the principalities and powers defended by spiritual wickedness in high places.

Nobody is going to be allowed to treat the working people like dogs and say:" we have an economic revolution."

No one is going to impose financial burdens on the people and say:"this is socialism."

The people are prepared to work but not for Bookers and Other Exploiters.

Forward to People's Power. Down with Suga Powa.

Trespass Cases Dismissed

Before Magistrate Mr. Satharan Singh the Squatters Norman Willins and Brother Harris were freed on a charge of Trespass. The prosecution could not say to whom the land they squatted on belonged. This means that the action of the police in arresting the men was unlawful. The Magistrate said that he did not award costs against the police because the police were obeying instructions. Legal opinion is that the police can be sued. A charge against Harold Thomas was also dismissed. Mr. CML John represented the squatters. It would be a pity for innocent policemen under orders to be made to suffer.

The Declaration of Bachelor's Adventure
ASCRIA
(Redemption Day, February 18, 1973)

The revolutionary people of this land, farmers without land, landless and homeless families, workers by hand and brain, revolutionary elements of the great African and great Indian people and other Guyanese are gathered together here on this day which we have called the Day of Redemption. Many are absent from this embankment but are present with us in spirit. We know this because the heart of the common people has always, and will always demand social justice.

Why are we here? What is our purpose? Some have said that our purpose is to overthrow the government. The government is being overthrown every day from inside. Every corrupt Minister, every Party activist who exploits the people every one in authority who exploits women, or exacts from wages of the poor for Babylonian banquets, these are overthrowing the government daily. It need not look outside for enemies. They are a multitude inside it. What then is our purpose?

The government has proclaimed an economic revolution. We

have stood aside and looked on at this so-called revolution. The government has proclaimed socialism and an egalitarian society. We have stood by and looked on, at this so-called socialism and so-called equality. What do we see? The gaps between the better off and the poor are getting wider. Unemployment remains a serious problem. Some people are given jobs lasting a very short time. People must submit themselves to get a job. Girls must consent. Collective punishment is imposed on certain organizations and certain villages because they contain people who expose the fraud of the so-called revolution. Villagers continue to be burdened with rates of all kinds. The line between the haves and have-nots is now sharper than ever. Ordinary people are pursued, hunted, and victimized by the party machinery for failing to obey, to submit, to toe the line. Looking back, we should not be surprised. You cannot put capitalist hustlers to build socialism. You cannot expect people who live by privilege to carry out a social revolution, or to uphold republicanism and equality. We are convinced that only a revolutionary approach to our economic resources can feed the hungry, end unemployment, and set at liberty them that are bruised.

Are we to stand aside and shut up when we see people preaching equality and practicing accumulation; preaching socialism and practicing capitalism; preaching tightening the belts and gorging themselves with plenty? The country is run in the supposed interests of the privileged few. The few are now more than before. They are African and Indian, Chinese and European, but they are few. They are the political elite, the managerial class in all sectors, and the higher party activists.

The masses have not enjoyed any improvement in their dignity, self-respect or social, material, or spiritual well-being. On the sugar plantations, the Africans have long been a mere minority. The Indians there are suffering increasing unemployment and increasing exploitation and are fighting it in various ways. The

Africans outside of the plantation are living through the same rising unemployment, lack of involvement in business, crushing local taxation without relief, and with the Indians, an acute land hunger for housing land and for well drained, or any fertile, agricultural land. Whereas a sizable number of mainly Indian families were settled in Black Bush during the PPP regime, no Black Bush has been created by the present government as a base for African agriculture. These are the things we are fighting to overthrow, not a government. Those who say we have no right to mobilize the people to overcome these ills are denying us our rights under the constitution of Guyana.

It is known that the ruling clique, for example, wear beards and dashikis. Yet anyone outside of that circle who wears beards or dashikis is harassed and called ASCRIAN and looked upon with suspicion. Any sister who wears *iro* and *lappa* is noted for future reference.

In the same way, the ruling party is really saying to us that they have an economic revolution and that we must be satisfied with the way it is going. If we try to take a revolutionary initiative, we are to be damned. This is not a healthy mentality. It is a mentality of fearful people afraid of their own shadows. Well, are we to apply for police permission to launch a drive in the interests of the people?

If we raise the burning question of corruption, we are told that we are splitting the race, rocking the boat, attempting to form a party and overthrowing the government. If we criticize the way Carifesta was organized, we planning to overthrow. If we raise the question of feudal capitalism, we are again said to be overthrowing the government. Everything is regarded as a personal attack on the Prime Minister.

The Land Movement says the *New Nation*, was planned between ASCRIA and the PPP—as the PNC themselves planned the nationalization of DEMBA with the PPP. They argue that the plan was to promote violence by the police and bring down the government. Stupid people, fumbling with matters. The only way a land squatting movement could bring down the government was if it was planned to happen at the same time as an army or police revolt. But the same *New Nation* makes it clear that there was no such thing planned and is yet saying that the Land Movement was planned to bring down the government.

We are standing on sacred soil. In the year 1812, dozens of African slaves were gunned down by Sugar on this land. In 1948, five Indian workers were gunned down by Sugar, not by the police, at Plantation Enmore, a mile away. The modern political movement derived much of its awareness from the Enmore shooting. We must no longer say that Indian workers were shot by African policemen but that Indian workers were shot by Sugar. From this embankment, we greet our Amerindian brothers and let them know that the same principles of equality and vigilance can help our relations. The Enmore shooting woke up everybody against the colonial system. But that impulse, for various reasons, did not result in a lasting people's victory.

The bussing off of Bachelor's Adventure in 1917 has not yet been corrected. Bookers took the land away by transport and we want it back, ALL of it, by transport.

ASCRIA happens to be an African organization concerned with the historical scars on the whole personality of African people. This campaign makes it clear that our organization is not aimed against the races of Guyana. We want a fraternal alliance among all who suffer and are heavily burdened.

In the People's Committees which developed out of the Land Campaign we see the most remarkable thing on the East Coast which became caught up in racial violence in 1963 and 1964. Continuing to place blame is at this point useless. The People's Committees have advanced beyond that stage. The People's Committees and the Council of the Landless Peoples are the only organizations in this country which are *truly interracial,* truly representative of the havenots and in which there is no power politics, no attempt at power politics, which can defeat attempts at inter-racial conflict and maintain revolutionary peace against the enemy, the exploiter. In the peoples committees, the Indian and African comrades discuss things frankly, and have no fear of one another.

We have fooled around in unstable equilibrium for many years. We do not believe that race is a dirty word. It is only when it becomes an instrument of exploitation and internal or international power politics. The Land Campaign must end in justice for the squatters and the principles of equality which they proclaimed, upheld and are still upholding. It is not our first such campaign, nor will it be the last.

Long Live The Martyrs of the Great African People!

Long Live the Martyrs of The Great Indian People!

Long Live the Peoples Committees and the Council of Landless People!

Let us Continue to Deepen the Revolution.

Resolutions Passed
Rally Called by Peoples Committees
of Lusignan, Annandale, Buxton at Annandale
(March 10, 1973)

Be It Resolved:

1. That this rally calls upon squatters to keep vigilant, and calls upon government to scrap plans for police McClean to victimize squatters and give land to favorites, and demands that first priority must be given to landless squatters.

2. That this rally supports the immediate transfer of Sugar In-

dustry Labor Welfare lots to the Lease holders at no cost.

3. That this rally demands a free transfer of land or transfer with no further payment to landless squatters on Sugar lands at West Lusignan.

4. That plans to build an airfield for the use of golf players from Georgetown and Berbice be scrapped and the land be given to the landless.

5. That the Guyana government collect an extra levy from exported sugar for the Sugar Industry Labor Welfare Fund whenever the world market price is at a level about 25 pounds sterling a ton and so stop the feudal capitalists from pocketing all the gains.

6. That this rally demands that non-resident sugar workers and cane farmers without any delay or postponement, and after years of promises and lies, be at once allowed to enjoy the benefits of the Sugar Industry Labor Welfare Fund.

7. That cane farmers share in the Canadian rebates of over half a million dollars total, of which cane farmers are entitled to a share. They must be paid at once since cane farmers cannot allow industry or government to owe us for three years. The pushing around should stop at once.

8. That this rally condemns the brutal killing of Brother Winston Hosannah at Vigilance and calls upon you to watch all who try to bring about a return to racial violence. We welcome the solidarity shown by cane cutters with his family, urge greater support and pledge to make a big collection next week.

9. That this rally again condemns the Government's failure to take back from Bookers the Bachelor's Adventure lands and the government's promise to give more lands to Bookers for Sugar lands.

People Force PNC to Pay for Sugar Lands
ASCRIA Drums: March, 1973
30 Street, Georgetown, Guyana

Read the following portions from the Prime Minister's speech on February 23rd, on Republic Night:

"…Government has been in discussion with the principles of such owners and made it clear to them that prices have to be reduced to what is reasonable in all circumstances. If they do not accept this position your government will have no alternative to legislation, for it cannot sit idly by and see the little man priced out of the opportunity of building and owning shelter over his head. It cannot permit wanton and unjustifiable inflation."

"… Those discussions, which were very detailed and intricate, and which ultimately embraced questions related to the expansion of the production of sugar, had already reached an advanced stage by December 1972—in fact they were almost completed—when some, whose vaulting political ambition is the only quality they possess, sought to disrupt these discussions by playing on the real needs of some of our citizens. It is my duty to announce that this morning Bookers signed a Deed of Gift transferring to the government free-of-cost all surplus sugar lands not beneficially occupied."

The Prime Minister makes three main points: First, that the government had been, since April, 1971, in discussion with Bookers about Sugar lands, "and made it clear to them that prices have to be reduced to what is reasonable in all the circumstances." Second, that politically ambitious people "sought to disrupt these discussions" – by launching the land seizure campaign calling on workers and farmers to seize sugar the sugar lands. Third, that by Republic anniversary night, February 23rd, all talk of "reducing" prices of sugar land became so shameful that the heirs of the slave owners (Bookers) and the heirs of the slaves (the government) has to stop it altogether. The campaign, "Not a cent for sugar lands" had won.

Discussions were going on about buying over sugar lands "at reduced prices." Then ASCRIA launched a public campaign. Then the *people* waged the campaign—Africans and Indians. Then the PNC government attempted to crush the campaign. The PNC denounced the campaign. Then the PNC left off all talk about paying Bookers prices, even "reduced" prices for land. The PNC and its government were forced for the time being to give up their shameful plan to help Bookers loot the country. That is what the plan was.

The peasant revolt against feudal capitalism and the methods of fighting used forced the government to make some actual changes in feudal landholding in the place of promises to cancel plans for paying money to Bookers for sugar lands. The PNC hypocrites are now saying, "It's a people's victory." Why then did Dr. Reid on January 22 serve 48 hours notice on the squatters with the bluff, "Government is taking possession…?" Why then did the government send hundreds of policemen to seize and burn shacks and to arrest squatters? Why did they have the "people's" army, the GDF, standing by for action against the people?

Burnham had to try to prove to the people that he is not a stooge of feudal capitalism—Bookers. So he made a deal with Bookers to save face. But in return, Bookers is given full freedom to win back the lands and to exploit the country—helping the PNC to build imperialist socialism:

"For our part we will ensure that sugar is allowed, encouraged—indeed spurred—to expand its production and make a definitive contribution to the employment and feeding of our people and to the growth of our economy. We are prepared to give leases to Bookers to expand cane cultivation in the normal way as is done for agricultural development—while insisting that such lands as come under such leases are promptly used for sugar cultivation. We will enter into consortia in which we have the majority holding in new and large scale development, and we will ensure that at all times sufficient land is reserved and available for the expansion of peasant cane farming (Mr. Burnham, February 23, 1973)

To keep the people of Bachelor's Adventure quiet, the PNC is giving them trench digging jobs which may last a few months. Bur Burnham has refused to take back from Bookers for the people at Bachelor's Adventure the land which Bookers stole from them in 1917. According to him, "The Cooperation from Bookers is heartening." And the Chairman of Bookers said: "We have no problem with the Guyanese government." He added this is strange in the Third World. And the cane farmers are offered Bookers lef-lef.

The Colonial Development Corporation Chairman, Sir Eric Griffith, boss of Guyana Housing Development Corporation was very pleased to find "socialist" government in Guyana that consents to their exploitation of the middle income middle class people in South Ruimveldt Gardens. He promises more financial exploitation for Guyana. The "socialist" government's Chronicle reported him as saying: "The Prime Minister and I have a very close identity of views"—that is, they think the same way. Mout

Open, Tory Jump Out!

Robert Hamer, boss of USAID, has said publicly that he is very pleased with how Guyana is going. He regards Guyana as a model for other countries. Why not? Recently, we entertained 100 and more white American businessmen from Indiana with V.I.P. treatment including a glittering reception at the PM's residence. This is a month after the government deported two highly principled Pan Africanist Afro-Americans from Guyana.

Burnham believes that $50,000 a year to the Freedom Fighters in Africa will cover a multitude of political sins. Guyana is proud to make that contribution, but it cannot excuse the government's cheap living-home with the enemies of African Liberation. The Chinese leaders, anxious for Third World company in their living-home with Nixon, are showering praise on Guyana for its "fight against imperialism." (*Peking Review* #37 and Chou En Lai's Republic Greetings, 1973)

So we are housing ourselves by 1976 with the kind aid and vicious exploitation of CDC's Guyana Housing. Our self-reliance development plan will borrow at least $500 million in foreign loans. If this self-reliance what is not self-reliance?

When people raise questions about the exploitation of the people and pseudo sham socialism, they are said to be "in the way of the revolution" and the *Evening Post*, that dog with its tail between its legs, eggs on the government to speed up its known plans for detention.

This is a strange revolution. The imperialists capitalists all support it and pray for it to continue. But the masses are bawling out for an end of exploitation and corruption, for an end to games and poses that must be exposed.

A revolution is not a revolution unless it restores the people's dignity. The unemployed men who must become slaves to get a job have no dignity. The young women who must pay with their bodies for jobs are slaves again. This is not a new life. It is the old life with new slogans.

WICKED LIES

The PNC, still secretly crushing the land campaign, is accusing large numbers of people of "joining" ASCRIA. This organization suspended "joining" over three years ago.

For Further Reading
on the History and Politics of Guyana:

Sara Abraham. *Labor and the Multi-Racial Project in the Caribbean.* Lanham, MD: Lexington Books, 2007.

Aubrey Armstrong, ed. *Studies in Postcolonial Society – Guyana.* Nashville, TN: African World Press 1975.

Frank Birbalsingh. *The People's Progressive Party: An Oral History,1950-1992.* London: Hansib, 2007.

Frank Birbalsingh. *Guyana and the Caribbean.* West Sussex, UK: Dido, 2004.

Forbes Burnham. *A Destiny to Mold: Selected Speeches.* New York: Africana Pub. Corp., 1970.

Norman Cameron. *The Evolution of the Negro.* Demerara, Guiana: Argosy, 1934.

Jan R. Carew. *Fulcrums of Change.* Trenton, NJ: African World Press, 1988.

Jan R. Carew. *The Guyanese Wanderer.* Louisville, KY: Sarabande Books, 2007.

Martin Carter. *Poems.* Oxford: MacMillan Education, 2006

Leo A. Despres. *Cultural Pluralism and Nationalist Politics in British Guiana.* Chicago: Rand McNally, 1967.

Kean Gibson. *The Cycle of Racial Oppression in Guyana.* Lanham, MD: University Press of America, 2003.

Norman Girvan. *The Caribbean Bauxite Industry.* Mona, Jamaica: (I.S.E.R.), University of West Indies, 1967.

R.A. Glasgow. *Guyana: Race and Politics Among Africans and East Indians.* The Hague: M. Nijoff, 1970.

J.E. Greene. *Race Versus Politics in Guyana.* Kingston, Jamaica: UWI – ISER, 1974.

Guyana: *Fraudulent Revolution.* London: Latin America Bureau, 1984.

David Hinds. *Ethno-Politics and Power Sharing in Guyana.* Washington, DC: New Academia Publishing, 2011.

Percy C. Hintzen. *The Cost of Regime Survival.* New York: Cambridge UP, 1989.

Basil A. Ince. *Decolonization and Conflict in the United Nations: Guyana's Struggle for Independence.* Cambridge, MA: Schenckman, 1974.

Cheddi Jagan. *Forbidden Freedom.* New York: International Publishers, 1954.

Cheddi Jagan. *The West on Trial: My Fight for Guyana's Freedom.* New York: International Publishers, 1967.

Henry B. Jeffrey and Colin Baber. *Guyana: Politics, Economics, and Society Beyond the Burnham Era.* Boulder, CO: L. Rienner Publishers, 1986.

George Lamming and Martin Carter eds. Guyana Independence Issue. *New World.* 1966.

Harold A. Lutchman. *From Colonialism to Co-operative Republic: Aspects of Political Development in Guyana.* Rio Piedras: University of Puerto Rico, 1974.

Robert H. Manley. *Guyana Emergent: The Post-independence struggle for non-dependent development.* Boston: GK Hall, 1979.

Perry Mars and Alma Young, eds. *Caribbean Labor and Politics: The Legacies of Cheddi Jagan and Michael Manley.* Detroit: Wayne State University Press, 2004.

Winston McGowan and James G. Rose. *Themes in African-Guyanese History.* 2nd Edition. London: Hansib, 2009.

Colin A. Palmer. *Cheddi Jagan and the Politics of Power: British Guiana's Struggle for Independence.* Chapel Hill, NC: UNC Press, 2010.

Ralph Premdas. *Party Politics and Racial Division in Guyana.* Denver, CO: University of Denver, 1973.

Shalini Puri. *The Legacies of Caribbean Radical Politics.* New York: Routledge, 2011.

Odida T. Quamina. *Mineworkers of Guyana: The Making of a Work-*

ing Class. London: Zed, 1987.

Stephen G. Rabe. *U.S. Intervention in Guiana: A Cold War Story.* Chapel Hill, NC: UNC Press, 2005.

Philip Reno. *The Ordeal of British Guiana.* New York: Monthly Review, 1964.

Walter Rodney. *A History of the Guyanese Working People, 1885-1901.* Baltimore, MD: Johns Hopkins University, 1981.

Euclid A. Rose. *Dependency and Socialism in the Modern Caribbean.* Lanham, MD: Lexington Books, 2002.

Maurice St. Pierre. *Anatomy of Resistance: Anti-Colonialism in Guyana, 1823-1966.* London: MacMillan, 1999.

Andrew Salkey. *Georgetown Journal.* London: New Beacon 1972.

David C. Scott. "Counting Women's Caring Work: An Interview with Andaiye." Small Axe. 8.1 (2004) 123-217.

Chaitram Singh. *Guyana: Politics in a Plantation Society.* Stanford CA: Hoover Institution Press, 1988.

Jai Narine Singh. *Guyana: Democracy Betrayed.* Kingston, Jamaica: Kingston Publishers, 1996.

Thomas J. Spinner. *A Political and Social History of Guyana, 1945-1983.* Boulder, CO: Westview Press 1984.

Clive Thomas. "State Capitalism in Guyana: An assessment of Forbes Burnham's Cooperative Republic," In *Crisis in the Caribbean.* Fitzroy Ambursley and Robin Cohen eds. New York: Monthly Review, 1983.

Ivan Van Sertima. *They Came Before Columbus.* New York: Random House, 1976.

Nigel D. Westmaas. "Resisting Orthodoxy: Notes on the Origins and Ideology of the Working People's Alliance." *Small Axe.* 8.1 (2004) 63-81.

Neil L. Whitehead and Stephanie Aleman eds. *Anthropologies of Guayana: Cultural Spaces in Northeast Amazonia.* Tucson: University of Arizona Press, 2009.

Other Titles Available From
On Our Own Authority!

Maurice Brinton -
The Bolsheviks and Workers' Control
1921 - 1921: The State and Counter Revolution

Kimathi Mohammed -
Organization and Spontaneity:
The Theory of the Vanguard Party and Its Application to the Black Movement in the US Today.

Lucy Parsons -
The Famous Speeches of the Eight Chicago Anarchists

Matthew Quest -
In the Shadow of State Power:
CLR James, Direct Democracy and National Liberation Struggles

Ida B. Wells -
Lynch Law in Georgia and Other Writings

For all questions regarding ordering, please e-mail us:
oooabooks@gmail.com

Visit us online:
www.oooabooks.org